WITHDRAWN

V O D O U

V O D O U

Visions and Voices of Haiti

by Phyllis Galembo

Introduction by Gerdès Fleurant

TEN SPEED PRESS

Berkeley, California

1☺

Ten Speed Press
P.O. Box 7123
Berkeley, CA 94707

Edited by Diana Reiss-Koncar

Additional text by Theodore Beaubrun, Marie Lily Cerat, Donald Cosentino, Gerdès Fleurant, Marilyn Houlberg, Serge Madhere, Elizabeth McAllister, Diana Reiss-Koncar, Sanba Grègory (Azouke) Sanon, and Sal Scalora

Text and cover design by Nancy Austin
Map page xvi by Diana Reiss-Koncar

Distributed in Australia by Simon & Schuster Australia; in Canada by Publishers Group West; in New Zealand by Tandem Press; in South Africa by Real Books; in the United Kingdom and Europe by Airlift Books; and in Malaysia and Singapore by Berkeley Books.

Printed in Korea

Library of Congress Cataloging-in-Publication Data on file with publisher

1 2 3 4 5 — 02 01 00 99 98

Photographs in preliminary pages:
Page i: Soukri, August 15, 1996
Page ii: manbo *(priestess) Jocelyne Louis Dalméus, dressed as Ezili*
Page vii: Gede, November 2, 1996
Page viii: Sodo, July 15, 1997
Page xi: Soukri, August 15, 1996
Page xii: mural depicting a vèvè *for Ezili*
Page xvi: Souvenance, March 30, 1997
Page xix: Soukri, August 15, 1996
Page xxi: Sodo, July 15, 1997
Page xxiv: Soukri, August 15, 1996
Page xxvi: Souvenance, March 30, 1997
Page xxviii: Souvenance, March 30, 1997
Page 1: St. Pierre, Port-au-Prince, November 3, 1997

CONTENTS

PREFACE

by Phyllis Galembo

Each November the Gede, the spirits of the dead, gather in graveyards around Port-au-Prince. In the sweltering autumn of 1996, I traveled to Haiti, intending to photograph these celebrations of the Vodou faithful. But on that occasion, for reasons unforeseen, I failed to capture the essence of the Gede ceremony on film.

One day that autumn, I found myself, camera in hand, among a whirl of worshipers crowded in a small public cemetery in Port-au-Prince. The graves had been recently weeded and whitewashed with chalk in preparation for the gathering of the Gede. Inside the graveyard, a crowd eddied around the chief Gede himself—the eerie, nasal-voiced Bawon Samdi. His physical features were those of Sauveur St. Cyr, a respected *oungan,* or Vodou priest, but the people in the cemetery understood that Sauveur had been "mounted" by Bawon—that he now embodied the spirit.

I had photographed Sauveur on numerous occasions, and on this day he invited me to attend a ceremony for Gede later at his *ounfò,* his Vodou temple.

During the rite, Sauveur appeared as Gede. Below his undertaker's top hat, his face was powdered skull white; cotton balls filled his eyesockets and the crease that was his mouth. I knew that Gede would die and be resurrected, and I'd planned to take his portrait as he lay prone upon the floor. But, as often happens in the course of my work, plans changed: Instead of taking pictures, I was told that my task would be to stand over Bawon and lift him from the dead.

When the time came, Sauveur's cousin took away my thirty-five-year-old Hasselblad camera for safekeeping; two young *ounsi,* or "wives of the spirits," struggled with armfuls of lighting gear; and, my hands now free, I linked Gede's little fingers with my own, raised my arms, and brought him to his feet.

Gede revived with flamboyant verve; hurling merry obscenities, he undulated through the crowd in his mock-sexual *banda* dance, gulping down *kleren* cane liquor. A spirit of the deceased, Bawon, with his wild gaiety, was turning death into satire before our eyes. For me the experience was one of many that showed how, in Vodou, incongruities do not seem to apply. This clowning, erotic Gede, whose symbol is a phallus, also holds the knowledge of the ancestors; a figure associated with graveyards, he is revered as the guardian of children.

* * *

Rags, clothing, costumes—my work has always focused on these elements. I'm fascinated by the way a piece of clothing can transform an ordinary person into someone magical, whether in the theater, in a holy place, or on the street. The portrait, too, has always been my favorite format, from the time I began photographing. I am especially drawn to figures that are costumed or in unusual environments, such as fantasy settings and theater tableaux.

In 1985, my work with such images led to an invitation from an artist and anthropologist to document altars and ritual dress of Edo priests and priestesses of Benin City, Nigeria. During the following nine years, I returned to Nigeria several times, attending rituals celebrating the *orisa* (deities). Photographing this material was a wonderful opportunity to explore my fascination with dress through the medium of the portrait.

In Nigeria, the use of ritual clothing continually captivated me. I spent four Christmas holidays documenting the custom of *aso-ebi*, or dressing alike, in which whole families don

matching outfits to show family solidarity and identity at communal celebrations. In 1997, with Nigerian writer Dympna Ugwu-Oju, I published *Aso-ebi: Cloth of the Family* with a grant from the New York Foundation for the Arts Catalogue Project.

In 1989, I began retracing the path traveled by Edo, Yoruba, Mande, Kongo, and Fon spirits to the New World as a result of the African diaspora. In northern Brazil, I photographed African-based Candomblé religious communities, hidden for centuries of slavery yet still flourishing. This vibrant Afro-Atlantic spiritual link became the theme of my 1993 photographic book, *Divine Inspiration: From Benin to Bahia* (University of New Mexico Press), an endeavor that brought together scholars and artists such as Robert Farris Thompson, David Byrne, Norma Rosen, Joseph Nevadomsky, and Zeca Ligièro.

* * *

Life cannot always be planned. As Vodou scholar and filmmaker Maya Deren has written, each of us serves in our own way. In my own case, I never set out to photograph Vodou. The desire to cross cultural boundaries and gain access to the unknown guided me. I was delighted when, over a cup of coffee in 1993, Donald J. Cosentino, curator of UCLA's sweeping *Sacred Arts of Haitian Vodou* exhibition, urged me to join the team from the Fowler Museum of Cultural History. I left that summer for Port-au-Prince with great excitement—and no idea what I would discover.

What I found was that in Haiti, African-originated Vodou religious beliefs are all-pervasive—they seem to be fused with the national history and culture in Haiti more than in any other country in the Americas. Common wisdom has long held that Haitians are "90 percent Catholic and 100 percent Vodou"—a fact that everyone from colonial slaveholders to modern church and state officials has steadfastly tried to suppress. If the people in these photographs surprise the viewer, perhaps it's because they reveal the hidden vitality of the Haitian Vodou tradition.

In Haiti, I recognized many of the Nigerian *orisa* that I'd seen in Nigeria, Brazil, and Cuba: Esu, the trickster messenger deity in Nigeria, is Exu in Brazil and Papa Legba in Haiti. Oxum, Brazil's vain and coquettish deity of fresh water, resembles Ezili, the Haitian goddess of love, who covets gifts of perfume and candy from her devotees. Ogun, the Edo deity of war and iron, aids taxi and tractor drivers in Nigeria. In Haiti he becomes Ogou, the warrior spirit of justice, and appears in the guise of the Catholic Saint James.

I began my search for Vodou temples, or *ounfò*, in Port-au-Prince, sometimes accompanied by art historian and anthropologist Marilyn Houlberg. In the neighborhoods of the city, we looked for flags that would signal the presence of an *ounfò*. Finding one, we would talk with the *oungan* or *manbo*—the priest or priestess—who, if they were inclined, would knock several times at the door of the *badji*, or altar room, to ask the *lwa*, or spirits, if I could be allowed entry. Once inside, I was invariably amazed by the creativity of the practitioners, and the tenderness they expressed for the *lwa*.

I've seen just as intense a devotion to the *lwa* in the beautiful and harsh Haitian countryside—domain of the farming deity Azaka—where Vodou flourishes as well. Visiting the plunging waterfalls at Sodo, far from the chaos of the capital, I witnessed a quarter of a million Haitian pilgrims who had come to bathe in the waters, which are considered magical. There I photographed worshipers shedding their ritual clothes in honor of the Virgin of Mt. Carmel, identified with Ezili Dantò, a mother-warrior spirit. Amid the falling water, *oungan* and *manbo* with their brooms cleansed the faithful in rituals that produced states of ecstasy.

* * *

I'm often asked how I make contacts in the course of my travels: Most are made by word of mouth, or through spontaneous meetings. I always search for an assistant from the place I'm visiting, and I've been fortunate to have some incredibly skillful people working with me. They are often rich sources of contacts themselves, and they also help me interpret languages and messages and arrange permissions from state bureaucracies and religious officials. In Haiti, translator Jean Marie Bien Aimé and I spent weeks rambling through the neighborhoods of Port-au-Prince; François St. Fleur helped me in the countryside.

When photographing people wearing ritual dress, I am almost always doing so *away* from the religious rites where that clothing is usually worn. The process of setting up a portrait shoot is interactive. People being photographed choose how they want to present themselves. They may not actually own the suit they wear, but borrow it from someone else for the portrait. Some might prefer not to be photographed alone, so they bring along a companion. As we prepare together, there's often a sense that this is a very important occasion.

As I work, my curiosity drives me on; but I remain mindful of the ethical questions: Chiefly, when, as a photographer, are you taking advantage of your subject? What's given is a gift, and the responsibilities involved in photographing rituals and ceremonial objects are many.

Above all, I try not to be a touristic voyeur, but a sympathetic participant and documenter. In the course of arranging photographic shoots, I try to develop a dialogue with the members of the community and their leaders. This close personal interaction often develops into relationships I retain for many years, and also a greater sense of community obligation on my part. As a photographer who is often tied into the fabric of a community, I have been generously allowed to photograph in the most intimate and sacred of settings. And there are also times, as at the Gede ceremony in Port-au-Prince, when I have to literally put my camera aside in order to participate.

* * *

As a visual artist, I am fascinated by the beauty that survives amidst the poorest slums on the planet—of which Haiti's rank high. On a crumbling shantytown wall ripples a vivid portrait of the serpent Danbala, spirit of wisdom, the life force, and ancient knowledge. From a crumpled pile, a man lifts a crimson rag; on his body, it transforms him into Ogou Feray, a soldier spirit battling miserable conditions. These ordinary objects, under the hands of human beings, produce magic.

You don't always see the magic or the beauty unless you know how to look. In Haiti, I went searching. The photographs in this book, taken between 1993 and 1997, represent the fruits of my search: They are not a complete picture of the practice of Haitian Vodou, but rather they accompany my own discoveries. The writings that appear alongside the photos were selected or commissioned to illuminate the photographs. I hope that these photographs and writings evoke for you the spirit of this fascinating and beautiful tradition.

ACKNOWLEDGMENTS

The first people to encourage my travels to Haiti were Donald J. Cosentino and Marilyn Houlberg, in 1993 when they were organizing the exhibition *Sacred Arts of Haitian Vodou* for the Fowler Museum of Cultural History in Los Angeles. Other supporting members of the museum were Doran H. Ross, David Mayo, Fran Tabbush, and Henrietta Cosentino.

Michele Rubin, my agent, and Amy Berkower at Writers House made the project possible by finding Ten Speed Press to support this work in grand style. At Ten Speed, Phil Wood decided to publish my project and was most generous; Clancy Drake edited, organized, and coordinated the project; Nancy Austin, among other things, provided the excellent designs in the book; and Diana Reiss-Koncar was Wonder-woman, organizing all the pieces into a flowing, readable text. It has been a delight to work with Ten Speed.

To Gerdès Fleurant, I am most appreciative for providing the introductory essay, for his encouragement throughout the project, and for providing additional material throughout the book.

While in New York, Sarah Farsad assisted me on a weekly basis, trying to keep me organized, David Yih provided invaluable help with the Kreyòl and other matters, and Marijo Dougherty, Shelley Rice, and Christopher Winks were always willing to lend a hand reading the manuscript. Axelle Liautaud and Chantal Regnault were always willing to answer my questions about Haiti.

Additional thanks in the United States go to Suzanne Preston Blier, Lisa Brewer, David Byrne, Dr. Kevin Cahill, Rachel Crognale, Allen Harris, Ronit Leora, Enid Shildkraut, Randall Morris and Shari Cavin, C. Daniel Dawson, Miriam Jacobs, Mel Rosenthal, Phillip Retzky, David Zaza, Lilly Lack, Brian Morissey, Jeanne Melillo, John Mason, Bill Hunt, Anne Turyn, Robert Farris Thompson, Eva Sutton, Edwidge Danticat, Mary Virginia Swanson at Swanstock, Lynne Warberg, and Marcia Lippman.

Contributors to the text include poets, musicians, writers, artists, anthropologists. Thank you to Henry John Drewal, Alison Laird Craig, Elizabeth McAlister, TontonGuy, Sivera Simon, Chantal Regnault, Karen McCarthy Brown, Serge Madhere, Carrol F. Coates, Sal Scalora, Gina Cunningham and Tap Tap Restaurant, Marie Lily Cerat, Anna Wexler, Theodore and Mimerose Beaubrun of Boukman Eksperyans, Peter Savanstano, Cheryl Ito, Sanba Grègory (Azouke) Sanon, Lois Wilcken, and Henry Claude Nelson.

To my friends who loaned me camera equipment and assisted me in Haiti helping me to make it happen, I say thank you: Joan Hackett, Mark McCarty, Daniel Morel, Tina Girouard, Jacques Pierre, Carry Jean, Ronald Derenoncourt, Rachel Beauvoir-Dominique, Veronique Lériche, Marianne Léhman, Matteo Lorenzo Marignoni, Jean Marie Bien Aimé, Alenord J. Baptiste, François St. Fleur, Richard Morse at the Oloffson Hotel, members of the Rasin Roots, Franck Désiré, Dieuseul Liberus, and the Department of Tourism in Haiti, especially Alix Lafond, Maryse Pennette and Suzanne Sietz.

Financial assistance for the project was received from the University at Albany, State University of New York, through a Senior Faculty Research Award and a Faculty Research Award and the New York Council for the Arts, Individual Artists Grant 1996. Several of my colleagues, Eloise Briere, Joanne Carson, David Carbone, Roberta Bernstein, Barbara Hackel, and Mary Osielski, were there for me.

To Rhoda and Norman Galembo and my family for their ongoing support in all my endeavors—thank you.

To the people of Haiti, who opened the doors for me, thank you for allowing me and my readers access to these most sacred spaces.

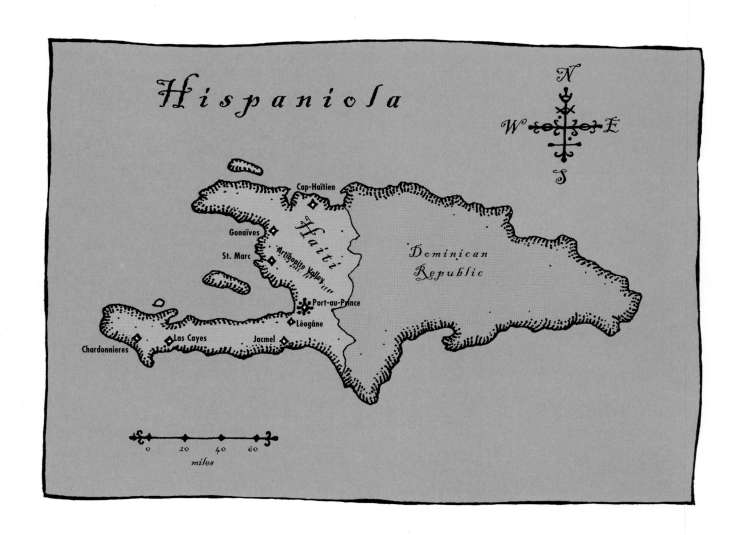

*I*n 1492, an errant Italian explorer sailing a Spanish ship bound for the unknown landed on a verdant stretch of Caribbean island he christened La Isla Española (Hispaniola). Though Africans arrived in the Americas along with Columbus's first voyage, the year 1502 is commonly cited as the official entry of African slaves into Hispaniola. Uprooted from their villages and cities on the Gulf of Guinea, they were brought in to replace the island's vanishing Taino-Arawak, whom the Spanish had quickly dominated and enslaved. With them, the Africans brought their religion, Vodou, and the historical memory of home it sheltered and preserved.

In the year 1697, after decades of small skirmishes launched from a neighboring islet, a company of French pirates, adventurers, and scrappy cacao and cotton farmers took over the western third of the island, leaving the eastern region, today's Dominican Republic, to Spain.

In the following century, the slave trade to Saint-Domingue burgeoned to accommodate the voracious needs of the sugar plantations, displacing millions of Africans from their native lands. Consequently, although born of three sources—African, Amerindian, and European—Haiti emerged as a nation whose African contributions form its principal cultural traits. And it is in this landscape that one must situate the history and the art of Vodou presented in this book.

* * *

The history of Haiti is also the story of its inhabitants' resistance to both physical enslavement and cultural oppression. Colonial laws that legalized the ownership of human beings

*V*odoun is clearly more than the ritual of the cult temple. It is an integrated system of concepts concerning human behavior, the relation of mankind to those who have lived before, and to the natural and supernatural forces of the universe. It relates the living to the dead and to those not yet born. It "explains" unpredictable events by showing them to be consistent with established principles. In short, it is a true religion which attempts to tie the unknown to the known and thus create order where chaos existed before.

—HAROLD COURLANDER,
The Drum and the Hoe: Life and Lore of the Haitian People

and their brutal exploitation on the sugar plantations of Saint-Domingue also banned any slave meeting—day or night—and saw to it that ethnic Africans were systematically intermixed so that any recollection of language, lineage, and ties to the motherland, known as Ginen, would be permanently lost.

A turning point in this saga is the 1791 Bwa Kayiman Vodou ritual and political congress held near Cap Français by runaway slaves. The gathering led to a general slave uprising, which became a war of national liberation that culminated in the proclamation of Haiti's independence on January 1, 1804. For the African captives who revolted, success was due in large measure to the cohesive force of Vodou—the religious cement that not only bound together a diverse range of ethnic peoples from Africa, but inspired them in their common strike for freedom.

Popular labeling of Vodou as "witchcraft" and "magic" has been a historical tradition among European colonialists—beginning with the early Saint-Domingue clerics and continuing with nineteenth-century propagandists, such as Spencer St. John, who could not make their peace with an independent Black nation. Today, Hollywood films and supermarket tabloids sustain these same popular myths.

Yet Vodou is essentially a monotheistic religion, which recognizes a single and supreme spiritual entity or God. This entity is known as Mawu-Lisa among the Fon people of West Africa, Olorun among the Yoruba, and Bondyé or Gran Mèt in Haiti. Besides Vodou's visible cultural and ritual dimensions expressed through the arts—especially in Haitian music and dance—its teaching and belief system include social, economic, political, and practical components. Today, for example, Vodou's basic teachings are concerned with what can be done to overcome the limiting social conditions of Haiti—a country whose people have been strenuously challenged from within and outside its borders: what to do in case of illness in a country that counts only one physician for 23,000 people, what to do before embarking upon major undertakings, such as marriage, business transactions, or traveling abroad. Vodou gives its adherents positive means to address these issues. In this regard, Vodou is a comprehensive system of knowledge that transcends the simplistic images—such as sticking pins into dolls, putting a hex on an adversary, or turning innocents into zombies—with which the popular media identifies it.

The primary source for Haitian artistic

expression, Vodou resulted from the fusion of rituals and cultural practices of a great range of African ethnic groups—most prominent among them, the Fon, Yoruba, Ibo, Hausa, Ewe, Kongo, and Toma Guinea. Scholars have called African culture "additive," in the sense that many African ethnic groups readily adapt foreign elements into their culture. Following the same pattern, Haitian Vodou absorbed many aspects of Catholicism into its ritual.

There are two main reasons for the appearance of Catholic elements in Vodou. The first was a simple matter of force: Colonial policies such as the Code Noir, or "Black Code," prepared in France in 1685, declared that "all slaves on our islands will be baptized" and that "the practice of all religion except Catholicism" would be forbidden. The second reason was appropriation: Presented with images of Christian saints, the Africans readily recognized in them elements that appealed to their own sensibility. In popularly accessible chromolithographs, for instance, Saint James the Greater, clad in steel armor, reminded them of Ogun, the Nigerian deity of war and ironsmithing.

This phenomenon is known as *syncretism,* and its meaning is the subject of serious debate among Vodou scholars today:

While some hold that Catholic practices were actually absorbed into Vodou, others contend that the Africans never accepted the European elements into their rituals and instead simply used the saints and Christian rituals as a cover to continue their own Vodou practices. Whether one accepts one interpretation or another, however, syncretism is a basic part of Haitian Vodou.

The phenomenon of syncretism can be observed in the prayer Dyò, an obligatory sequence recited in song at the beginning of all Vodou ceremonies. The prayer begins with a call to "Grand Père Eternel," or God, continues with the Lord's Prayer, the Hail Mary, and the Apostles' Creed, and goes on with an acknowledgment of all the known male and female Christian saints. Though many of these saints have no corresponding Vodou *lwa,* their names are called anyway, for Vodou is inclusive and the practitioner would rather err on the side of inclusion than risk offense. The next section of the prayer Dyò is devoted to the calling of all the African and Haitian *lwa* in the precise order received from African tradition. The prayer concludes with a call to all unknown saints, spiritual entities, ancestors, or departed family members whose names have not been mentioned. In this manner all the "bases" are covered, for the totality and integrity of nature are paramount in the Haitian conception of the universe.

It is interesting to note that in the past ten years, with the advent of the "root culture" movement driven by the progressive wing of culturalists (Vodou organizations such as Zantray, Bòde Nasyonal, New Rada Community, and the Congress of Santa Barbara, which emerged around or after the fall of Duvalier in 1986), efforts to drop the first part of the prayer Dyò have been resisted by many *oungan* and *manbo* (priests and priestesses), who contend that it is part of the tradition and that they see no need to do so, since such a modification would not, in their minds, amount to a substantial change.

* * *

In colonial Haiti, the Africans came into contact with the original inhabitants of the island, the Taino-Arawak and the Carib. In time, the captives would also adapt elements of indigenous ritual into their own Vodou practices. This can be observed in the Vodou practitioner's use of polished stones, considered sacred, and also in symbolic ground drawings, called *vèvè* or *seremoni*, indispensable at all rituals (particularly elaborate ones like *kanzo* and the *boule zen*, during which

initiates are subjected to the rite of fire). The *vèvè* are also in part the legacy of certain African ethnic groups, such as the Edo of Nigeria, who use them in the same manner as Haitians do: Each *lwa* has an intricate *vèvè* design that recalls its unique characteristics.

Before the arrival of the Europeans and Africans, the original inhabitants of the country called their island Bohio, Haiti, or

Quisqueya. In Taino-Arawak, Haiti means "mountainous land," a name that attracted the attention of the African independence fighters, for the country's topography accounted in a large measure for their victory over the French.

* * *

As practiced in Port-au-Prince today, many Vodou ceremonies conform to one of two major rites: The Rada rite retained from the old kingdom of Dahomey (comprising parts of present-day Nigeria, Benin, and Togo) is generally agreed to be most faithful to West African tradition. The Petwo rite is a newer development that arose out of the crucible of the New World plantation system and encompasses elements of the Kongo culture as well as the practices of many other groups from Central Africa to Angola in the southwest.

The Rada rite is Vodou's most elaborate rite and includes the great communal spirits or *lwa,* such as Atibon Legba, Marasa Dosou Dosa, Danbala and Ayida Wèdo, Azaka Mede, Ogou Feray, Agwe Tawoyo, Ezili Freda Daome, Lasirenn and Labalenn, and Gede Nimbo. It is generally assumed, by Vodou practitioners and researchers alike, that the

Rada *lwa* are *dous* or sweet. These *lwa* represent *flè Ginen,* the "flower of Guinea" or true spirit of Africa, and are the first to be saluted at Vodou ceremonies. Their sense of justice is well developed, as they promote the concept of spiritual balance of both the individual and the collective. They are first and foremost the profound and traditional mysteries of Africa, the foundation of the principles by which all in the community live.

Contrary to popular conception, the line between Rada and Petwo *lwa* is not as rigid as it appears: Much of what is described as Rada goes for Petwo. Yet, many Vodou practitioners maintain that the Petwo *lwa* are *anmè,* or bitter. Associated with fire, the Petwo spirits are said to be *lwa cho,* or hot *lwa,* engaging in violent behavior. The Petwo rite includes major *lwa* such as Mèt Kalfou, Simbi Andezo, Ezili Dantò, and Bawon Samdi, to cite the best known. Some of the *lwa*—said to exist *andezo,* or in two cosmic substances—are served in both Rada and Petwo rituals.

The *lwa* are the intermediaries between humans and the realm of the spirit. Among the most important belonging to the Rada are Atibon Legba, Marasa Dosou Dosa, Danbala and Ayida Wèdo, Azaka Mede, Ezili

Freda Daome, Agwe Tawoyo, Lasirenn and Labalenn, Ogou Feray, and Gede Nimbo. On the Petwo side of the equation, the major *lwa* include Mèt Kalfou, Simbi Andezo, Ezili Dantò, and Bawon Samdi. As spiritual entities, the *lwa* symbolize major forces and elements of nature—such as earth, water, air, fire, wind, and vegetation—as well as human sentiments and values, such as love, bravery, justice, and fidelity.

Atibon Legba, which means "tree of justice" in Fon, is the spirit of the crossroads; his effigy was found by all crossroads and

open doorways in Dahomey. As an intermediary, Atibon Legba links the *lwa* and the humans and opens the cosmic gates through which all energy must pass. He is saluted first, before a Vodou ceremony can proceed. His symbols are the cross and the crutch that he uses to support himself, and Atibon Legba also symbolizes old age, respect, and wisdom, as expressed in the following well-known Kreyòl song:

> *Papa Legba nou vye*
> Father Legba, you are very old
>
> *Atibon Legba nou vye*
> Atibon Legba, you are very old
>
> *Se pa jodi-a ou gran chimen*
> Forever you have been the highway
>
> *Atibon Legba nou vye*
> Atibon Legba, you are old indeed

Mèt Kalfou is the emanation of Atibon Legba in the Petwo rite, and shares with him similar characteristics in Vodou liturgical practices.

Danbala and his cosmic wife, Ayida Wèdo, form together an organic whole. Represented by two snakes that symbolize the principles of fertility and flexibility of matter, they are among the oldest entities of

Vodou rites. Danbala means "in the house of Dan" in Fon; Dan is the royal serpent, the founding ancestor of the lineage, the symbol of the kingdom of Dahomey. Danbala and Ayida Wèdo greet the Vodou assembly, here referred to as Kreyòl, in this song that reminds them of their African origin:

> *Kreyòl bonswa Danbala Wèdo*
> Kreyòl, Danbala Wèdo salute you
>
> *Kouman nou ye*
> How are you all doing?
>
> *Danbala Wèdo reponn*
> Danbala Wèdo answers
>
> *Nou la ye*
> We are fine
>
> *Ayida Wèdo reponn*
> Ayida Wèdo answers
>
> *Nou la ye*
> We are fine
>
> *Kreyòl Danbala nou ye*
> Kreyòl, we are Danbala

Ogou Feray is the principle of defense and war. The Ogou consist of a family of ironsmith-spirits from Yorubaland, now part of Benin and Nigeria. The Ogou also embody the principles of medicine, pioneering, and intellectual exploration. Therefore, anything having to do with tools that can advance humans' mastery over the environment falls within their purview. In Haiti, there are many manifestations of Ogou that are worshiped in both the Rada and Petwo rites. They are known under names such as Ogou Badagri, Ogou Balenjo, Ogou Batala, and Ogou Je Wouj. The Ogou are among the guardians of the *badji*, the altar in the sacred chamber of the *ounfò* or Vodou temple, as expressed in the song below:

> *Feray-o, lan men ki moun*
> O Feray, in whose hands
>
> *Ou kite bagi-a la*
> You left the watch of the *badji*
>
> *Lè m rete m sonje Ogou Feray*
> When I remember Ogou Feray
>
> *M a konsole m m a pran kouraj-o*
> I'll console myself and take courage

Ezili Freda Daome, the cosmic counterpart of Ogou, is the embodiment of love, feminine beauty, coquetry, wealth, and good luck. The principle of motherhood, as well, Ezili is manifested in three aspects: Ezili Freda in the Rada rite, lighter in complexion and conflated with the Virgin Mary; Ezili Dantò in the Petwo rite, darker in complexion and assimilated with Our Lady of Mount Carmel (the Black Madonna); and Grann Ezili, the synthesis of the previous two, symbolizing the principle of feminine wisdom and maturity. The most recognizable symbol of Ezili is the heart.

Ezili may possess men as well as women, and the same can be said for Ogou, who may mount or "possess" a woman also. In fact, most *lwa* do not discriminate when it comes to communication with the community: It does not matter if the body is that of a man or a woman. Ezili, the epitome of community welfare, is solicitous of the needs of the people, as evidenced in the following song:

Ezili Freda
Ezili Freda

Pale ti moun-la-yo
Tell all the children

Ezili Freda rele miwazan-e
Ezili Freda call the community

Gen youn tan ou a sonje m
It's time for remembrance

Ezili gets her name from Nigeria, where the river Azili can be found. Therefore, in Haiti, she is said to reside in the water as the guardian spirit of rivers, and in this regard, Lasirenn, the mermaid, and her sister Labalenn, the whale, are other emanations of the same spirit. In Haitian Vodou legends, Lasirenn, a light-colored woman, sits by the river combing her long hair with a golden comb, which if found by a human being— usually a man—will make him rich. However, to catch such a prize can be dangerous, as noted in the following song:

Lasirenn Labalenn chapo m
Lasirenn Labalenn my hat

Tonbe lan lanmè
Fell in the sea

M ap fè bèbèl ak Lasirenn
I was flirting with Lasirenn

Chapo m tonbe lan lanmè
My hat fell in the sea

The man's hat fell in the sea—it is understood that he may soon follow.

Lasirenn is also known as one of the cosmic wives of Agwe Tawoyo, the spirit of the sea who protects seafarers and reigns over the ocean. His symbols are the conch shell and the miniature boat often seen hanging over a beam at the *peristil* or dancing space of the Vodou temple. Agwe's other cosmic partners are the Ezili. An elaborate ceremony at sea is conducted in their honor every twenty-one years.

The principle of Agwe Tawoyo is continued in the personage of Simbi Andezo, or "Simbi in two waters." While Agwe Tawoyo presides over the ocean, Simbi Andezo is the lord of fresh waters found in waterholes and rivers. Though served in both Rada and Petwo rites, Simbi Andezo is one of the most powerful Petwo *lwa*. His relation to Danbala and Ayida Wèdo, the primordial water spirits, is expressed in the song below:

> *Simbi Dlo ou ale*
> Simbi of Waters, you have left
>
> *Danbala Wèdo ou ale*
> Danbala Wèdo, you have left
>
> *Simbi ou poko konnen mwen*
> Simbi, you don't know me yet
>
> *Simbi Dlo ou ale*
> Simbi of Waters, you have left

Marasa Dosou Dosa enjoys an eminent place among the *lwa*. The word *Marasa* is a contraction of *Mawu-Lisa*, the name of the primordial supreme being of the Fon of Dahomey, but in Haiti Marasa has become the child spirit of the twins, and is conflated with Saint Cosmas and Saint Damian. The words *dosou* (male) and *dosa* (female) complement Marasa with a third entity considered to be the child born before or after the twins. Thus in Haiti, one speaks of *marasa twa*, or "twins of three." According to legend, Saint Nicholas (or, alternatively, the sun) put the children back together after they were cut up by a butcher, and is said to be their father. In some parts of Haiti, the Marasa are saluted before Legba. Their tremendous gift of clairvoyance is indicated in the following song:

> *Genyen je o Marasa layo*
> You have eyes, Marasa
>
> *Genyen je o genyen je o*
> You have eyes, you have eyes
>
> *Pou nou gade yo la*
> To see through everything

Azaka Mede, the deity of agriculture, whose symbols are the straw sack and the sickle, is well known in Haiti, for he represents the essence of an agricultural country. He carries the dignified title of Minister (Mede) of Agriculture, stressing the importance of his role. Yet he is also known as Kouzen Zaka, which indicates he is the cousin or brother of the common person. In addition, he is referred to as *flè Vodou* (flower and quintessence of Vodou) and

lewa (the king). The term *gweli-o*, often found in songs to Azaka, makes allusion to his sickle, an important instrument of the Haitian peasant. Songs to Azaka, such as the following one, are accompanied by *djouba/matinik*, a rhythm well known in the Americas, particularly the United States, and associated with the plight of the common people:

> *Azaka gweli-o*
> Azaka with your sickle
>
> *Azaka gweli-o*
> Azaka with your sickle
>
> *O minis Azaka Mede*
> O minister Azaka Mede
>
> *Na wè sa*
> We will see a better day

Finally, Gede Nimbo, the head of one of the most numerous families of *lwa*, is the principle of life and death, and as such governs the cemeteries. The Gede are the protectors of children, and in this sense they complement Atibon Legba, the spirit of the beginning. Among the Gede one finds the well-known Bawon Samdi, the lord of the cemeteries, often represented dressed in black mourning coat and top hat (a legacy of

song below tells the story of a group of Gede who at carnival time insisted that they be received at the National Palace in Port-au-Prince, thus symbolizing the right of the common people to political recognition.

Papa Gede bèl gason
Papa Gede handsome man

Gede Nimbo bèl gason
Gede Nimbo handsome man

Abiye tout an blan
Dressed all in white

Poul al monte opalè
To enter the National Palace

Lè l abiye tout an nwa
When dressed all in black

Li sanble youn senatè
He looks like a senator

Lè l abiye tout an blan
When dressed all in white

Li sanble youn depite
He looks like a congressman

* * *

Masonic symbols), holding a *baton zaka* or baton of Azaka in one hand, dancing to the semicomic and sexually provocative rhythm of *banda*. Other symbolic implements of Bawon Samdi are the shovels, coffins, skulls, and skeletons seen in many images that represent him in this book.

While songs to Gede are often lewd, the Gede as entities are among the most instrumental *lwa* of Vodou, for they are politically active in the affairs of the community. The

The Vodou ceremony consists of a series of songs and dances accompanied by the drums, offered in honor of the *lwa*. The music and dance of the Rada rite is the *yanvalou* (meaning "invocation" in the language of the Fon/Ewe), and always appears with its dance complements, *mayi* and *zepòl.* Together, they form what I call the "*yanvalou* trilogy." In effect, *yanvalou,* a solemn rhythm that is played on a battery of three drums of different sizes, guided by the linear rhythm of an iron bell called an *ogan* and played in $^{12}/_{8}$ time, is de rigueur in all Vodou ceremonies. It is followed by *mayi,* the heavy-foot dance of the Mahi people, neighbors of the Fon of West Africa, and the *zepòl* (from the French *épaules,* or shoulders), a shoulder dance that in many respects resembles the fast *agbekor,* a dance/music of the Ewe people.

At ceremonies conducted in the Petwo rite, the people play and dance *petwo,* which is comprised of two major musical variants, the *kita* and the *boumba,* representing the respective music traditions of these Kongo and Central African peoples. The *kita,* played faster, is composed of short dry strokes and sequences that emphasize the upper sound register, while the *boumba* calls for more melodious sound in the lower register. *Petwo,* in both its *kita* and *boumba* forms, is danced upright, with alternating foot movements.

Possession, an important dimension of Vodou worship, is among the least understood aspects of the religion. Through possession, both the *lwa* and the community are affirmed. The people transcend their materiality by becoming spirits, and the spirits renew their vigor by dancing and feasting with the *chwal,* or horses, for it is said that during possession the *lwa* rides a person like a cavalier rides a horse. Equally as important, possession is a time when the *lwa* communicate in a tangible way with the people, who during such times receive the best possible answers to pressing questions. The frantic crises that are pictured in Hollywood horror films rarely come to pass. When they do occur, it is most often to those called *bosal,* or noninitiates, who have not yet learned to sustain the weight of *lwa,* for during possession a person experiences a displacement of *gwo bon anj,* or "big consciousness," which is taken over by the *lwa.*

At ceremonies, Vodou practitioners include the *ounsi* or initiates—known as the children of the *lwa*—the *andjennikon* or chorus leader, the *laplas* or sword bearer, the *ountò* or the drummers, the *oungan* and *manbo,* the priest and priestess. There are three levels of *konnesans* or esoteric knowl-

counseling, they often do this through divination. For that purpose, they use playing cards that they spread in a *laye* or large straw tray. Some practitioners are able to divine solely by using a lit candle and a glass of water.

Vodou's liturgical calendar parallels the Roman Catholic one, but rituals can be held at most times of the year, depending on the needs of patrons or members of the community. Notable dates are the November 2 Feast of Gede, a time to remember the dead and the ancestors; the *pile fèy* from December 24 to January 6, which centers around the crushing of leaves with medicinal properties to make ritual baths; and the Holy Week to Easter Sunday *rara* celebration, when reveling musicians, members of a Vodou temple, and the *rara* kings and queens, dressed in elaborate sequined costumes, travel about the countryside to perform for the community and dance in front of the homes of influential patrons. One of the most elaborate ceremonies is the *boule zen,* the burning of the pot mentioned earlier, performed at temple dedications and other solemn occasions throughout the calendar year. Key Vodou ceremonies, however, are never held during Lent, for it is a time of revitalization, charged

edge in initiate matters. The *ounsi bosal* has not learned yet how to negotiate the path of knowledge. The *ounsi kanzo* is an initiate who has gone through a rigorous learning process, which includes the manipulation of fire during ceremonies called *kanzo* and *boule zen* or "burning of the pots." The *oungan* and *manbo* have achieved a higher degree of *konnesans* in ritual matters and, therefore, officiate at ceremonies and minister unto the people. In addition to everyday with powerful spiritual forces that cannot be easily calmed.

What is the future of Vodou in Haiti and outside, in the diaspora? Haiti's recent 1987 constitution recognizes freedom of religion in Haiti and Vodou as the national religion of the Haitian people. Yet Vodou continues to endure an ambivalent status in Haiti, for many attempts have been made to uproot it. While such purges have generally failed, they have the effect of casting doubt on its merit as a cultural practice. The Haitian educational system, for example, which favors a cosmopolitan approach, has yet to include the study of Vodou mythology in its curriculum.

During the past thirty years, however, people have been practicing Vodou openly. Today's Haitian expatriate community (also known as the Tenth Department, since Haiti's territory is divided into nine departments) numbers over a million Haitians. The diaspora includes many Vodou advocates, including respected artists and writers like Frankétienne and world-renowned musical groups such as Boukman Eksperyans, Boukan Ginen, RAM, and the Fugees. The University of California at Los Angeles's *Sacred Arts of Haitian Vodou* ex-

hibition constitutes one more effort in a series of activities aiming at fostering better understanding of Vodou. Finally, the 1997 congress held at the University of California, Santa Barbara, where Haitian scholars and Vodou practitioners met to discuss the role of Vodou in the development of Haiti, hopes to function as a guide and resource center for providing accurate information on Vodou from an insider's perspective.

Finally and importantly, no single person or organization has the final word on Vodou—a complex system of universal knowledge and cultural practices inherited from Africa and brought to the New World. With its decentralized structure, Vodou has been diffused throughout Haiti, growing and transforming to meet the needs of the people and the existential realities of the land. Thus Vodou, the rich cultural heritage of the Haitian people, far from being a form of superstition, remains the true source igniting and inspiring the country's artistic expressions—as evidenced in this book. With its reverence for the ancestors, Vodou is the cement that binds family and community life in Haiti.

Note on Orthography and Kreyòl

Within the written contributions to this book, the reader will encounter a range of spellings of the word *Vodou* (*vodun, voudoun,* or *voodoo*), as well as related terms. Alternate spellings of words that appear in this book are listed in the glossary alongside the preferred spellings. With a few exceptions, spellings in this book follow those in Albert Valdman's *Haitian Creole–English-French Dictionary.*

Until the early 1980s there was little consensus on the orthography of the Kreyòl language, the tongue spoken by almost the entire population of the country. Today most contemporary scholars use the spelling *Vodou*—instead of the once-popular *voodoo*—to salute the historical roots of the religion and to convey its evolution from Africa to Haiti, but also to distance themselves from the general tendency of foreigners to devalue Haitian culture. The word *Vodou* itself comes from the Fon language and means "ancestral spirit and drums." Today, *Vodou* is the generic term for all aspects of the sacred ritual of the Haitian people.

In Vodou parlance, many other African and Kreyòl words are readily encountered. Most of the African words are retained from the Fon, Ewe, Kongo, Yoruba, and other languages spoken by the ancestors of today's Haitians. To refer to a specific spirit, for example, Haitians used the Kongo word *lwa.*

The Kreyòl language has a life story of its own. Now spoken by the Haitian people (80 percent of whom have been kept in a state of chronic illiteracy by the elite minority), Kreyòl grew out of seventeenth-century French grafted onto a West African syntax base. In Kreyòl grammar, the article follows the noun, plural words do not take an *s*, and past tenses are constructed according to context, rather than with the termination of the verb, as in French. Kreyòl is essentially a spoken language, though it has evolved into a full-fledged written medium.

Through incantation, prayer and proverb, Vodou and Kreyòl are intricately linked. Indeed, Vodou's wisdom is preserved through the oral tradition inherited from Africa and developed in the new context.

V O D O U

Lwa

SPIRITS

*T*he *lwa* are supernatural beings that can enter the human body, and they are thought to be present in all realms of nature: in the trees, the streams, and the mountains; in the air, the water, and fire....The spirits provide a way of classifying the different provinces of the universe, as well as of life in society. Order and disorder, life and death, good and evil, favorable and unfavorable happenings—all take on meaning through the agency of the *lwa*, leaving nothing to strike the faithful as absurd.

—LAËNNEC HURBON, *Voodoo: Search for the Spirit*

Manbo (priestess) Nini Pierre-Louis wears the ritual dress of the lwa *Bosou. One of the central practices of Vodou is spirit "mounting"—when the* lwa *enter the body of a priest or priestess in order to communicate to the faithful.*

2

Legba
Keeper of the Spirit Gate

Lord of the gate between the spirit and material worlds and divine messenger to the gods, Legba appears as a ragged old man hobbling on crutches. Usually honored first at Vodou ceremonies, he must open the barrier to allow the faithful to invoke the other *lwa*. Associated with saints Peter and Anthony and the color red, Legba possesses his spiritual "horse"—the person whose body he enters—with great force, and he enables the lame to walk.

Atibo Legba, open the barrier for me,
Papa Legba, open the barrier for me,
To let me through,
When I come back I will salute the *loa*
Voodoo Legba, open the barrier for me,
When I return, I will thank the *loa*.

—ALFRED MÉTRAUX,
  Haiti, Black Peasants and Voodoo

* * *

*Detail of a mural depicting Legba
and a drummer.*

For anyone on a long journey like yours, Legba, the spirit of the highway, is the most important *vodoun* of all. Remember that any crossroad is a very dangerous place. It is there that the force of Legba is strongest. From the crossroad, every direction but one is wrong. Legba can help you or hinder you. If he feels like it he will send you the wrong way and perhaps you will never be able to return. If you come to a crossroad and your direction is not clear to you, make his sign in the dust and call his name. You can call him Legba, Attibon, Eshu, or Master of the Highway.

—KUKU CABRIT, in Harold
  Courlander's *The Bordeaux Narrative*

4

*In this photograph, Mihenle, an oungan (priest), is possessed by Papa Legba,
protector of the home and guardian of gates and crossroads.*

Ezili

Spirit of Love

Ezili moves in an atmosphere of infinite luxury, a perfume of refinement,
which, from the first moment of her arrival, pervades
the very air of the *peristil* and becomes a general expansiveness
in which all anxieties, all urgencies, vanish.

—MAYA DEREN

This is how ethnographer and filmmaker Maya Deren describes the way the spirit Ezili manifests herself in a Vodou ceremony. The *oungan* or *manbo* (priest or priestess) has a big supply of perfumes that he or she generously and continually sprays on all the people who attend a ceremony for Ezili.

Manbo Esperancia Federic, a Vodou priestess of Jacmel (pictured on page 7) has made "spirit marriages" with three Ezili spirits of love. After these spirit marriages, they will all protect and empower her in various ways. The spirits of Ezili range from the coquettish Kreyòl, light-skinned Ezili Freda, to the tough, resilient Ezili Dantò, to Ezili Je Wouj (literally "Ezili Red Eyes"), considered the most dangerous of the three. To a certain degree, they represent aspects of womanhood in a universal sense, aspects that are reflected in the spirit beliefs not only in Haitian Vodou but in many religious traditions. Women can

sometimes be romantic, sometimes hardworking mothers and providers, and sometimes jealous and dangerous.

Manbo Esperancia first married Ezili Freda, the Kreyòl spirit of love, in 1959. Ezili, who loves luxury, is represented here not only by the perfumes on Esperancia's altar but by the Catholic chromolithograph of the Virgin Mary, bedecked with jewels, the largest chromolithograph above the altar table. Ezili Freda is considered to be a gentle, seductive *lwa* in the Rada tradition of Vodou. Her colors are pink and white, just like Esperancia's bedspread. Her favorite foods, served in her honor, are light in color and usually sweet. They frequently include rice cooked in cinnamon milk or bananas fried in sugar. She likes sweet drinks made with orange syrup or grenadine. If she smokes, her cigarettes are mild, like Virginia Slims. Her favorite perfume is Anaïs-Anaïs

Manbo *Esperancia Federic, a priestess from Jacmel, dressed as Ezili, sits
in her bedroom shrine for Ezili. Appropriately, she has an array of
perfumes, which Ezili loves, on the altar table next to her bed.*

Mural of Ezili Dantò, who is associated with Our Lady of Mount Carmel, or the Black Madonna.

by Cacherel, the label of which is pink and white on a white bottle.

The next Ezilis Esperancia married were Ezili Dantò and Ezili Je Wouj, both "hot" Petwo spirits associated with the color red. She married them in the same ceremony since, as she put it, they *"mache ansann"* (walk together). The rose-colored satin dress,

red scarf, and red shoes worn by Esperancia and the red Vodou bottle she holds all relate to Ezili Dantò and Ezili Je Wouj.

Petwo divinity Ezili Dantò is a hard-working and fiercely protective mother; her child is said to be a daughter, Anaïs. She is represented by the chromolithograph of the Black Madonna and child. Dantò is associated with the indigenous black pigs of Haiti and with tough country ways. She is said to raise pigs in her rural realm and thus her favorite food is fried pork *(griyo)*. Her scent is Florida water. Her favorite drink is the strong Barbancourt rum. If she smokes, it is unfiltered Camels or strong Haitian cigarettes.

Ezili Je Wouj ("red eyes") takes her name from the fact that when she manifests in a ceremony, her devotees, while in trance, rub red pepper in their eyes. She is powerful and dangerous and can accomplish much for her followers.

All of the Ezilis are said to require their devotees to be very clean and "fresh." *Manbo* Esperancia is a prime example of this. Her clothes, in their plastic dry cleaning bags, connote this principle. The whole shrine is crowned with Christmas garlands and even includes a Christmas tree, al-

*Mural of Ezili Freda, who is associated
with the Virgin Mary.*

though this photograph was taken in July.
    Manbo Esperancia takes great solace and
power from her Ezilis and they have helped
her through some personal tragedies. In
turn, she has created a tribute to them in the
form of this intimate bedroom shrine.

—MARILYN HOULBERG

* * *

REMINISCENCES & VISION

Erzulie the coquette, charming soul,
shining beauty with a terrible spell
is the goddess of love, smiling power.

Dragon saint of all sexual prowess
defender of women's mysterious glory
guardian and mother of the land
she covets tenderness, celestial
    fulfillment
in a life of tears and betrayed desires.

She is my mother and lover and
    wonder
the sun from the darkened horizon
the light through the tunnel of pain
she is Erzulie my sweet *compañera*
the transcendental link between horror
and Bad-life perturbed in non-sense;

Erzulie the coquette, charming soul
has filtered the air with powerful magic.

—TONTONGUY, *The Vodou Gods' Joy*

* * *

Seven stabs of the knife, seven stabs of the sword.

Hand me that basin, I'm going to vomit blood.

Seven stabs of the knife, seven stabs of the sword.

Hand me that basin, I'm going to vomit blood.

So sings Ezili Dantò, the black Madonna of love, as she manifests in a Vodou ceremony in Karen McCarthy Brown's *Mama Lola: A Vodou Priestess in Brooklyn. Manbo* Iguelida of Jacmel is shown here (page 11) in the red and blue colors of this dangerous Petwo spirit. As a *manbo,* the powerful Vodou priestess of an *ounfò,* or temple, she holds the *ason,* the rattle that is the symbol of her office.

As her song indicates, Ezili Dantò has strong powers and can protect her followers, or "children," from any harm. Those who would do damage to her devotees have to deal with the stabbing of the knife and the sword. Dantò's song demonstrates her profound power, so strong she can vomit blood at will. *Manbo* Iguelida leans up against the *poto mitan,* the centerpost of the temple through which the *lwa,* the spirits, are said to travel up and down as they communicate between the spirit world and the mortal world.

Manbo Iguelida's husband, Lemaire Ridore, is an *oungan* dedicated to Ogou, a Vodou warrior spirit who, as shown here, is represented by a machete or sword and the color red. Ogou, a West African military spirit associated with iron and war, is credited with helping Haiti become the first Black independent nation in the Western Hemisphere, in 1804. *Oungan* Lemaire Ridore takes a tough pose, complete with cigarette. Together as mortal husband and wife, they officiate over their *ounfò* in Jacmel. However, they also reflect the cosmic marriage of the two *lwa,* Dantò and Ogou, who work together in the spirit world as husband and wife and provide powerful protection for their spiritual followers.

—Marilyn Houlberg

Wall painting of Ezili Je Wouj,
a fierce manifestation of Ezili.

Manbo *Iguelida and* oungan *Lemaire Ridore as Ezili Dantò and Ogou.*

Ogou
Spirit of Iron

The Ogou are a family of spirits embodying the principles of intelligence, pioneering, and justice. They are known under such names as Ogou Feray, Ogou Badagri, Ogou Batala, and Ogou Je Wouj. Ogou is associated with fire and rum and carries an iron saber and a red sash. Ogou is also the *lwa* of power, authority, and triumph; the means by which these are achieved vary historically, and today Ogou often takes the form of a political figure.

The crusader Saint James the Greater, who vanquished the Moors, is identified with Ogou Feray, the warrior hero, spirit of justice, and protector of the Vodou community.

Ogou master of fire, master of iron,
  Nago man,
Ogou no-nonsense.

* * *

What could we do without you, Ogou?
How could we go to battle without
  you, Ogou?
And to win the battle, without you,
Ogou, we are nothing.

Saint James, Ogou Fè, Ogou Balendjo, Ogou Badagri, the whole Ogou family squad, Achadè, Chango, Saint John the Baptist, we respect you all.

Nago Fè, man of fire, man of war!

* * *

War against whom?
Against ourselves.
War against the old man in us,
war against exploitation,
war against all that shackles our mind.
War against all those who want to show us that the world is normal as it is, that pollution is normal, and selfishness
  is normal.

—THEODORE (LÒLÒ) BEAUBRUN

Oungan *Silva Joseph dressed as Ogou Badagri, in the uniform of a military general.*

Gede

Spirits of the Dead

Gede are the *lwa* of the dead; they hold the knowledge of the ancestors, and they are the guardians of children.

A vèvè (ritual drawing) for the Gede.

The people who created Guedé needed a god of derision. They needed a spirit which could burlesque the society that crushed him, so Guedé eats roasted peanuts and parched corn like his devotees. He delights in an old coat and pants and a torn old hat. So dressed and fed, he bites with sarcasm and slashes with ridicule the class that despises him.

But for all his simple requirements, Guedé is a powerful *loa*. He has charge of everyone within the regions of the dead, and he presides over all that is done there. He is a grave-digger and opens the tombs and when he wishes to do so he takes out the souls and uses them in his service.

Guedé is never visible. He manifests himself by "mounting" a subject as a rider mounts a horse, then he speaks and acts through his mount. The person mounted does nothing of his own accord. He is the horse of the *loa* until the spirit departs. Under the whip and guidance of the spirit-rider, the "horse" does and says many things that he or she would never have uttered un-ridden.

—ZORA NEALE HURSTON,
Tell My Horse

Bill Carzeau and Madame Micheline, Vodou priests from Port-au-Prince,
dressed as Gede Nimbo, guardian of children.

Vodou's spiritual entities are called <u>lwa</u>, from the Fon words <u>lo</u>, "mystery" and <u>lon</u>, "the heavens."

* * *

The "dead" spirit Gèdé Nimbo, the guardian or master of the cemetery, who often engages in bizarre activities which poke fun at the codes of social behavior, is sometimes regarded as a special protector of children. Precisely because he is overlord of all that has to do with the grave, his good will is sought, particularly in behalf of the young; and in many services of the Nago rites his protection is bought by money gifts.

Gèdé, take the money,
I will give you money, money,
I will give you money to guard
    the children!
I will give you money to guard
    the children!

—HAROLD COURLANDER,
*The Drum and the Hoe: Life and
Lore of the Haitian People*

*Oungan Sauveur St. Cyr poses as Gede
Janmensou ("Never Drunk") in front
of his altar to Gede.*

Bawon Samdi

Bawon Samdi is head of all the Gede. His symbols are skull and crossbones, graves, and shovels.

> Papa Gede is a handsome guy.
> Gede Nimbo is a guy.
> He is dressed all in black.
> He is going up to the palace.

Gede loves sun glasses. Because they look cool, of course, and in his own way, he's a chic *lwa*. Since the cemetery is his home, shades help him to see when he moves outside the gloom of the grave. Sometimes his glasses only have one lens. Some say one lens helps him to see both above *and* below the ground. Others say the glasses have one lens because the penis has one eye, and Gede is known as a dickhead. Or maybe the Ray Bans are a put-on of the Tonton Makouts, Duvalier's hated militia, who favored shades as an essential part of their gangster wardrobes. Gede loves to mock the powerful. As state authority has refined its mechanisms of oppression, so too has Gede sharpened his flip-off of established authority into elemental, and often hilarious, manifestations of the common contempt for brummagem civility. Gede is a bum, and all the more popular for his bad manners....Jean Philippe Jeannot's altar (pictured this page) reveals Baron Samedi's high status as a Freemason. Skeletal designs used in 32nd Degree initiation ceremonies, All-Seeing Eyes, skull and crossbones, funeral tools—these all belong to Baron as Grand Master of the celestial Masonic lodge of Vodou Heaven.

As for "Samedi," or Saturday, is it not the one day of the week when Christ remained in the tomb, the true day of the dead between Good Friday and the Resurrection on Easter Sunday? Baron Samedi is the divine pivot between the living and the dead.

—DONALD J. COSENTINO

Altar of Jean Philippe Jeannot.

Portrait of Jean Philippe Jeannot as Bawon.

Oungan *Celestin Montilas Philippe, a priest from Port-au-Prince, posed as Bawon Lakwa.*

Baron Samedi is a family man, presiding over a whole clan of related spirits who bear a startling collective resemblance to the Addams family. There is for instance Baron Lakwa, the imbecilic brother who keeps the cemetery grounds. Note his dashing black sports shirt, and the top hat inscribed with his own name and that of *zonbi*, those wretched living dead of Haitian folklore who are under the mystical supervision of the Baron. Lakwa is a ghoul who will kill on contract, and zombify for a price. But even if he kills, it is Gede who must dig the grave. And as Haitians insist, "If you do not merit death, Gede will refuse it."

—DONALD J. COSENTINO

Are there not several degrees of death?
Can death follow life, or is it not life
    that follows death?
How do we see death?
As an enemy or as a friend?

Death, is it not you who are the
    ultimate advisor?
Death, is it not you who are the
    real master?
It is only death that can grant us
    a reprieve.

We must die in ourselves.

We must die alive if we are to go
    through the doors of sound
to find the *pwen*, the point of power,
the formula, the essence of True Ginen.
The point that is beyond good and evil

Brave Gede, Gedelavi,
without you, without your order,
who can close the doors of the
    magic rite?
Who will go to the crossroads for us
    if it is not you,
Brave Gede, Gede Simityè, Gedelavi?

—THEODORE (LÒLÒ) BEAUBRUN

Azaka

Spirit of the Land

Identified with the Catholic Saint Isidore, Azaka is the patron *lwa* of farmers. With Saint Isidore's blue robe transformed into a denim shirt, Azaka carries a large *makout*, or straw bag.

Section of altar for Azaka in the ounfò *of Andre Chelemague, with the* lwa's *bag, or* makout, *in view.*

*P*ants and shirt made from karabel, a sturdy blue denim woven in Haiti; a *makout;* and a broad-brimmed straw hat—these make up the standard costume of Azaka, as well as the traditional garb of the peasant farmer in Haiti. It is partly because of such similarities in clothing that Azaka came to be identified with the Catholic Saint Isidore. In a chromolithograph widely distributed in Haiti, Isidore appears in blue pants and cape, a sack slung over one shoulder. The two are also connected by the agricultural theme: in the lithograph, Isidore kneels in prayer while behind him, an angel plows the land with a pair of white oxen.

—Karen McCarthy Brown,
Mama Lola: A Vodou Priestess in Brooklyn

*Oungan Castra Philippe poses by a mural of Azaka Mede, displaying
the symbols of bag, pipe, and denim clothing.*

*Azaka appears on the wall of an ounfò
in the guise of Saint Isidore.*

Kouzen Zaka, Azaka Mede, Azaka Tone!
He who is guardian of the farm, and the
    one who tills the land
Peasant spirit, who speaks the true
    language of the mountain
He who has the secret of the alliance
between the Arawak and the Africans.
Zaka, you are the true master,
you show us how to work,
how to reach the powers.

* * *

Oh Zaka, when will you make me hear
    all the sounds?
Oh Zaka, when will we resemble you?
Oh Zaka, how long, how long?

—THEODORE (LÒLÒ) BEAUBRUN

Portrait of Malant Pierre, of Léogâne, dressed as Azaka.

Lasirenn

Spirit of the Water

I am cold, I am wet
I have just come from the cold sea
I cannot stand up because half my body
    is a fish
Bring me my comb
Bring me my mirror

So sings the mermaid Lasirenn, a spirit associated with seduction and wealth. Her arrival is marked by the blowing of the conch shell, like the plaintive call of a foghorn. The *ounsi* (initiates) quickly come to the *lwa's* side, bringing her symbols—the comb and hand mirror—necessary accouterments for self-adornment. Supported by *ounsi* under each arm, Lasirenn gently swings back and forth, as if moving in deep water.

Slowly combing her "wet" hair, Lasirenn gazes into her looking-glass. For the Vodou practitioner, mirrors resemble pools of captured water and are associated with water itself. Both have reflective surfaces that can be used to communicate with other worlds. Water indeed enters Vodou cosmology in many forms and on many paths. Marine spirits such as Lasirenn can be contacted through bodies of water ranging from the sea to rivers and streams, to springs and pools—whether natural or in tubs in the Vodou temple. These spirits also animate the volatile elements of the tropical storm: the gusting winds that precede the rain, the thunder and lightning that accompany it, and the rainbow that marks its conclusion. Aquatic creatures such as fish, whales, and snakes, particularly the rainbow python, join fantastic creatures such as mermaids to symbolize the *lwa* of the water. In Haiti, the major female divinities—the Ezilis and others who "walk with" them—all are associated with water to some degree.

Wall painting of Lasirenn.

Ounfò of Blan Samdi Kriminèl in Jacmel.

Blan Samdi Kriminèl, an oungan *from Jacmel.*

The fishtailed Lasirenn, whose Kreyòl name derives from the French *(La Sirène)*, is sometimes known as Ezili of the Waters. She has the ability to bring riches and romance, but she can also be violent, and even has the power to lure mortals to a watery death. She is said to "seize" those who offend her—that is, those who do not honor contracts they made with her: promises of sacrifices and gifts made to Lasirenn in return for wealth, success in love, and the other blessings in life that she has the power to bestow.

In difficult economic times, practitioners particularly appreciate Lasirenn for the wealth she can bring—in today's Haiti, she plays an important role. Her image, with comb, mirror, and trumpet, is frequently painted as a wall mural in lottery parlors—and of course, on both the interior and exterior walls of *ounfò*, or temples.

The image of Lasirenn as painted by the *oungan* (priest) Blan Samdi Kriminèl on the wall of his small *djevo* (sanctuary room) in Jacmel, oddly enough, has no arms. Still, her hair is "wet," her scales are scintillating, and she has a prominent upturned tail.

Above her is a depiction of the water spirit Danbala and his wife Ayida Wèdo—

snake spirits represented by the rainbow python—which flank the *vèvè* (ritual drawing), for Ayizan (the *lwa* of initiation), a Masonic symbol. In the center of the interlocked *X*s is the Masonic eye, inside the *G*, which is variously said to represent geometry or God in his role as the master architect of the universe. To the right of Lasirenn is a large image of Danbala coiled around a palm tree and attended by an *oungan,* whose white hair indicates his wisdom and seniority.

The links between the rainbow python and the rainbow itself are many, and are found not just in Haitian Vodou but in cultures and belief systems in many parts of the world. Not only is the long shape of the imposing python the same as that of the arching rainbow in the sky, but the iridescence of its scales makes it appear that, as it moves, rainbows are flitting across the body of the snake. Rainbows link the sky with the land, the spiritual with the material. In Haiti, a double rainbow means that both Danbala and his wife, Ayida Wèdo, have come out together.

Both Lasirenn and Danbala are combinations of water spirits from diverse sources ranging from Europe and Nigeria to the Republic of Benin, formerly Dahomey, the home of the Fon. Today the Fon still paint the rainbow python Danbala on the sides of their Vodou temples. He is often depicted as a snake-headed rainbow with a pot of gold at the base of his tail, a sign of the wealth he can bring. In Vodou, Lasirenn and Danbala and his wife Ayida Wèdo all bring the promise of good things to come.

—MARILYN HOULBERG

Danbala & Ayida Wèdo
Snake Spirits

Some women marry a snake. After that they open a drawer every day and get money. Like there's this white girl as a matter of fact. She took a picture with a snake all over her. They say she had a baby and she couldn't find out who was the father. Do you know who I'm talking about—the one in the poster?

—Manbo Camille

A depiction of Moses (Sen Moyiz) in the ounfò of Raoul Louis San, in La Petite Rivière. Moses is associated with Danbala.

Visions, dreams, and mystical revelation illuminate the path of spirituality in the Afro-Haitian belief system. Just as many religious Catholics lead their lives with great sensitivity to the workings and interventions of their saints, so many adherents of Vodou interpret everyday events as mystical signs from the hands of the *lwa* who guide their lives.

Images from religion, art and popular culture can also signify the *lwa*. From the beginning of the colonial period, images in the form of icons of the Mother Church—both paintings and statues—made their appearance in Haiti. Gazing at these depictions of the saints, the Vodou faithful perceived mystical affinities between those holy Christian beings and the divine forces from Dahomey, Yorubaland, and Kongo. The *lwa* Danbala Wèdo lives "behind" Saint Patrick, who is depicted in Roman Catholic chromolithographs casting the snakes out of Ireland. Some say that Danbala's father is Moses, whose staff God turned into a snake when he threw it down before Pharaoh. These visual puns were mystical clues that revealed the saints to the early Africans, along with dreams and revelations.

When he possesses people, Danbala

*Portrait of Danbala Wèdo from an ounfò (temple) in Jacmel. According to Henry John Drewal, this image origi-
nated in a nineteenth-century chromolithograph poster advertising a snake charmer in Germany. Versions of
the image have appeared in West Africa, India, and the Americas: Here, the erstwhile snake charmer is identified as Reine Traveaux, "The Queen of Work." The snake is Danbala, and the inset signifies Ayida Wèdo.*

*Ounfò of Louis Marc Désir in Jacmel, with Danbala depicted in
the poster of Nastassja Kinski on the wall.*

Wèdo comes as a snake, moving them along the floor on their bellies, with both arms stretched out overhead. The congregation covers Danbala—in the body of the possessed person—with a white cloth, shaking it to cause a rippling movement that yields breezy energy. Then the spirit is presented with a single raw egg: elemental, whole food, a food containing life.

From the temples of Port-au-Prince to Haitian congregations in Miami and New York, a great number of women marry Danbala in mystical wedding ceremonies. On the day of the event, a special priest is hired to chant parts of the Latin Mass. A wedding license is drawn up; white cake is served. Rings are exchanged, and Danbala's bride wears a gold serpentine one on her finger. She also observes a vow of chastity each Thursday night. On this special evening, Danbala may come to visit her in dreams, where he appears in the form of a tall white man resembling Saint Patrick.

The 1981 Richard Avedon photograph of a nude Nastassja Kinski lying with a boa constrictor was a mass-produced poster in the United States. It became wildly popular, and was displayed everywhere from art galleries to private homes to dorm rooms to auto shops.

American celebrity photography depends on us—the consumers—knowing who celebrities are and valuing their image. When we buy their posters, we form an attachment to them, gazing at the image with pleasure and yearning.

Within Vodou culture and arts, people see, desire, and consume somewhat differently. When *manbo* Camille of Brooklyn saw this image, she didn't read it as a young actress set in a risqué pose captured by the highest priced fashion photographer. Nor did she see Kinski's body as the latest development in the female nude within the history of Western art. Camille did not note in the subject's horizontal face a reference to Man Ray's masks. She did not even read Eve and the Serpent.

Instead, the *manbo* read the image as an allegory about the mystical marriage to Danbala, a union which brings luck, money, and fertility. Indeed, such a spiritual union can even bring what the Catholics might label a miracle—a fatherless baby conceived by a snake.

—Elizabeth McAlister

Bosou
Bull Spirit

Bosou is a *lwa*, like Gede, who "walks as a family"—that is, there are a number of closely related spirits named Bosou. Some of them are understood to be Petwo or "hot" spirits, while some of them are Rada or "cool" spirits. Dyobolo Bosou, for instance, is a Rada *lwa* associated with water, while Bosou Twa Kòn is honored in the Petwo tradition. Bosou is often figured as a bull; he is a strong, warlike spirit who is prone to acts of violence, but who is also capable of good deeds. He may be decended from a bull spirit of ancient Dahomey who guarded the king of that land.

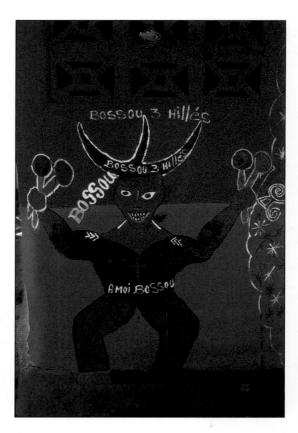

Bosou Twa Kòn on the wall of the ounfò *of Alexi Gangan Bienconnu in the Artibonite Valley, clutching* ason *in both hands.*

Mural with Bosou.

Altar to Bosou in the ounfò of oungan Pierre Ristil, town of Cannot in the Artibonite Valley.

Repozwa

SACRED PLACES

*V*odou's places of worship abound. Indeed, Haitian practitioners would say they are embodied in every corner of the earth. As with African traditions, there are no specific temples to Bondyé, or God, whose abode is the entire universe. Still the *lwa* are served in the *ounfò* or temple—often a covered structure with open sides. Separate closed chambers called *djevo* are reserved for the Rada and Petwo *lwa* respectively. At the center of the temple is the *poto mitan* or centerpost, the axis through which the *lwa* descend and possess the faithful.

Oungan *Guy of Léogâne posed as Bawon Kriminèl in an outdoor temple.*

Ounfò

Temple

The *ounfò* is the temple where Vodou worshipers perform ceremonies and rites. It contains sacred trees and the multiple structures—the altars, *peristil,* and small rooms—where the *oungan* and *manbo* cure those with illness, as well as sacred and ritual objects. The *ounfò* serves as a socioeconomic, productive unit where young people learn to farm, cook, sing, dance, and perform rituals to serve the spirits.

Within the ounfò *is where the* lwa *or spirits have their own huts known as* kay-mistè, *or "huts of the mysteries." These may also house personal possessions of the servitor, such as this refrigerator or this portable radio. In this sense, symbolism and practicality come together in a way that is often difficult for the outside observer to comprehend.*

Altar, interior of Bawon Lakwa shrine, Port-au-Prince.

Peristil
Dance Space

At the very edge of the *lakou*, or family compound, where I grew up, on the very shore of the Caribbean, stood our local *peristil*. The sacred structure was owned by a hardworking couple, a priest and priestess known simply as Jean and Manbo. It was primarily through their eyes and souls that I came to know Vodou, the religion that taught my ancestors and community self-discipline, self-worth, and self-esteem.

Jean, I remember, was seldom caught with his back to the sea. As an *oungan*, he knew that the Beginning and End are the same, and so he admired the undisturbed horizon, the blue water and sky that seem to leap into one another. It is a sight that makes the infinity theory comprehensible, for the boundary between the two is, after a long stare, indistinguishable.

Jean and Manbo's *peristil* also served as the place from which our community drew strength to survive: Children and adults in the compound went there for shade and repose. The building seemed always to have the space to accommodate the passing traveler, the pregnant teenager just thrown out of her house, or the unemployed laborer who could not afford sleeping quarters. Anyone in need, including those with what was called in whispers the "unmanly" or "unnatural" disease, found a home in the *peristil*. It belonged to the community; the door was always open.

If Vodou ceremonies are Haiti's public concerts, *peristil* are the country's dance halls. Anyone passing by and attracted by the sounds and vibrations of the drums is welcome. Here, young men get their first drumming lessons; talented young women may put on performances fit for the stages of Broadway; indeed, when the celebrated dancer and choreographer Katherine Dunham came to Haiti, she swore she witnessed the best dance steps in the island's *peristil*.

It's been said half-jokingly that if the Catholic church in Haiti gave away as much food as the island's Vodou *peristil*, the church would be able to claim a far greater number of adherents. It's not hard to understand why: Vodou ceremonies always include plenty of food—slaughtered goats, pigs, chickens are cooked and become offerings, either for thanking the *lwa* for a favor, or for asking them for protection. These foods are also offered to the hungry mortals who come to serve the *lwa*.

—MARIE LILY CERAT

Outside an ounfò or Vodou temple on the road to Carrefour, Port-au-Prince.

Ounfò Abandonnen
Abandoned *Ounfò*

Church and state eradication campaigns against Vodou practice began soon after African slaves landed in Haiti and continued throughout the colonial era. In 1896, the bishop of Cap-Haïtien condemned Vodou; it was responsible, he claimed, for "so many violations against the purity of the faith, so many offences to the saints, so many outrages against God himself," that "whatever the cost, we must get rid of this tumor; we must wage pitiless war against this army of brigands, the *bocors*, whose existence alone brings us disgrace."

Anti-Vodou crusades continued after independence and into contemporary times. In "The House," Haitian writer Sanba Grègory (Azouke) Sanon recalls a 1986 crusade, of which he and other worshipers were victims, and during which a number of people were killed. Here, he eulogizes both a lost comrade and a lost *ounfò*.

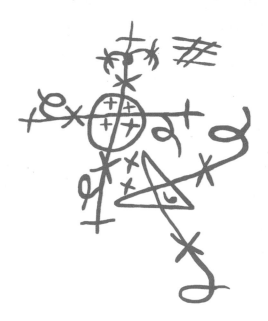

THIS HOUSE, THIS *OUNFÒ*!

Many *lwa* came from the four corners of the country to visit us, inside this small, rundown house. Inside this *ounfò*, we wrote poetry, composed songs, learned to dance, and talked politics. On our way, we lost one of our brothers who was very dear to our struggle. So from that day on we decided to move our house somewhere else. But the *lwa* still visited us wherever we were.

> Good times we're there.
> Bad times we're there.
> We will show them.

> Forget not the word we talked about.
> We must not forget the chat we
>   chatted about.

> I have this dog, they call it *"yabezwen."*

> I have another one
> They call it *"pa fè twop."*
> If they eat the neighbor's meat
> Just tell me, I'll pay for it.

> In the Latibonit Valley,
> There is a river that crosses over
>   its mother
> But does not cross over its father.
> *Ounsi* Kanzo, out of my way?

—SANBA GRÈGORY (AZOUKE)
  SANON

An abandoned ounfò *in the Artibonite Valley.*

Ounfò St. Louis Bata

St. Marc, seventy-five kilometers outside of Port-au-Prince, is known as one of Haiti's strongest centers of Bizango, a Haitian secret society. The temple of *bòkò* (sorcerer) St. Louis Bata, visible from the road, is one of a number of Bizango *ounfò* in St. Marc, and boasts a series of murals remarkable for their raw energy and directness. In these paintings, St. Louis, a self-taught artist, has created rectangular figures with thin, curving arms and tiny fingers.

Exterior, ounfò *of St. Louis Bata.*

Murals on the building's exterior feature the particular *lwa* (spirit) worshiped in the *ounfò*: Ezili Dantò, the Petwo spirit of love, here a Black Madonna and child flanked by the divine twins, the Marasa. An inscription atop the mural reads, "African twins of Ginen are reclaimed and born here," referring to the African source of the beliefs and rituals in Haiti that center around twins. Indeed, St. Louis himself descends from a long line of twins and triplets and salutes this illustrious heritage on a number of the walls of the three *badji*, or sanctuary rooms, as well.

St. Louis has inscribed on the walls of his *ounfò* all the services he provides to his clients. In a sort of illustrated price list, the *lwa* are shown surrounding amounts he charges. On the wall above St. Louis's name is an inscription, "Sonnin diable la $10.15," meaning "Ring for the devil here"—apparently affording the *bòkò*'s clients a chance to contact the devil for any number of reasons. Below this sign is another: "Chandele $7.20," advertising the candle-gazing ceremony in which practitioners predict the future and contact the dead. Beneath this sign sits a woven tray with playing cards for divination.

Murals salute Ezili Dantò, the black warrior-mother spirit, equated with the Christian Black Madonna, alongside a range

St. Marc. Wall paintings, ounfò of St. Louis Bata.

St. Marc. View of the altar at the ounfò of bòkò (sorcerer/priest) St. Louis Bata.

At a Petwo working table, the *bòkò* uses a candle lit on a human skull to contact the spirit of the cemetery, Bawon Samdi. To the right of the table, Bawon is represented in the form of a cross flanked by two rainbow python spirits—Ayida Wèdo and her husband Danbala. By gazing into the candle, specific people who have died can be contacted. They may complain of being wet, cold, and hungry through the guttural "death" voice of the *oungan* or priest; they may also request sacrifices and ceremonies if they are to ascend from the deep-sea waters, part of the journey of departed souls back to the ancestral home of Ginen.

Two plastic dolls tied at the neck repre-

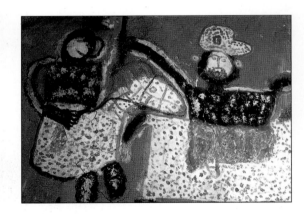

Depiction of Saint James the Greater, who is conflated with the warrior lwa *Ogou Feray.*

of Bosou representations. An inscription labels the large, three-horned Bosou Twa Kòn as "General Bosou." To his left floats a double-horned Bosou; to his right, an enigmatic head sporting an animal ear on one side and a five-fingered projection on the other.

sent Bosou, the bull spirit, and his wife. The necklace that joins them shows that, as St. Louis put it, "Unless you have both the husband and the wife working together, walking side by side, they can't do their work."

Bosou, a symbol of strength and power, is also represented by a pair of bull horns wrapped in the Petwo red cloth with a round mirror in the middle. Mirrors, with their reflective surfaces, are frequently used as an access point to other worlds and to spirits. Animal horns are said to have special powers not only in Haiti, but in many parts of Africa, where horns are often packed with magical medicines when they are prepared either for ritual work or to function as protective amulets. In this case, the horns of Bosou are suspended from the ceiling and twirl in the air as people pass by or a breeze en-

ters the altar room. Many other objects hang from the ceiling over the table covered with Vodou bottles, herbs, and candles. The melted wax on the table attests to its frequent use.

Leaning up against the wall, behind the Bosou couple and below the Catholic chromolithographs of the saints, are two red-cloth Vodou dolls—messengers to the world of the dead that do the bidding of the *bòkò* St. Louis on behalf of his clients. The death aspect of these two dolls is apparent in the white cotton filling their eyesockets, noses, and mouths, resembling the funerary practices for actual human corpses in the many parts of Haiti where people cannot afford embalming.

—MARILYN HOULBERG

Wall painting of Ezili Dantò.

Badji
Altar Room

How do artifacts link the worshiper to the world of the spirits? Altars in many cultures can be described as "cosmic cockpits," a term coined by Yale art historian Robert Farris Thompson. In the altar rooms of Haiti, *manbo* and *oungan* negotiate the spirit world, presiding over and manipulating a wide variety of sacred objects and artifacts as they serve their clients, members of their *ounfò*, and their families.

This altar in Jacmel, a small coastal town south of Port-au-Prince, is owned and was created by *manbo* Marie Guerda Simplice. It has a delicate, intimate ambience. *Pakèt kongo*, the spirit-activated healing bundles, line the left of the altar. To the right of the *pakèt* is a deck of playing cards used in divination.

Looming over the altar in the form of a softly rounded black-and-white cruciform is the ever-present spirit of death and the cemetery, Bawon Samdi. He is appealed to as a way to communicate with the dead and also as a way to stave off death, for he is a specialist in these matters. As is typical, on the wall above this crucifix hang chromolithographs of the Catholic saints equated with the various African-derived Vodou spirits. From left to right: Sen Jak Majè (Saint James the Greater) on his white horse, also known as Ogou, orig- inally the Yoruba/Fon spirit of iron and mili- tary might; Ezili Dantò, a spirit of love, also known as the "Black Madonna"; Saint Isidore, kneeling in a field, known as Papa Zaka, the Vodou spirit of agriculture and bountiful harvests. Below the chromolitho- graphs are *govi*, terracotta pots dressed in cloth that represent spirits of the dead. In front of the spirit pots are two *ason*, calabash rattles with beads, that are the essential sym- bol of Vodou liturgy. *Manbo* and *oungan* salute each other with their *ason* when they open any Vodou ceremony.

On the altar's right-hand side stands a dynamic little imported "action figure," dressed in red, the color of Ogou (and in- deed, Madame Simplice indicates that the figure is a tribute to that particular *lwa*). Here, the notion of "pumping iron" takes on new meaning, as the Vodou spirit of iron and military might is embodied in this commer- cially produced doll.

The base of the altar reveals a stylized representation of the Petwo spirit of love, Ezili Dantò: a heart and two daggers, sym- bolizing her fierce motherly love, with the Bawon Samdi's black-and-white cross re- peated in the center. It is a sensitive, tex- tured, and evocative representation mirror- ing the *vèvè*, a cosmogram for Ezili Dantò.

A complete badji or altar room inside the ounfò *Ja Cezir of* manbo *Marie Guerda Simplice, in Jacmel.*

Badji *in the* ounfò *of Jean Pierre. Danbala and Ayida Wèdo are depicted on the wall, as is Ogou.*

*Ounfò of Sauveur St. Cyr. This altar displays four
depictions of the Virgin Mary (associated
with Ezili Freda), as well as figures of Saint Isidore
(Azaka) and Saint James the Greater (Ogou).*

In front of the altar is a metal stand with a small bowl of stone ax blades, or "celts," immersed in oil. These Stone Age blades are activated or "charged" by setting fire to the oil and are considered to be the formidable tools of a number of *lwa*, including Ogou. In Nigeria, among the Yoruba, who use the blades in a similar fashion, the celts are said to be made by Ogun. The warrior spirit gives the blades to Shango, spirit of thunder and lightning and protector of the moral order. During storms, Shango hurls the blades down from the sky along the paths of lightening bolts to punish and kill liars and thieves.

This six-by-eight-foot *badji* or sanctu-ary is tiny, yet it has all of the requisite *lwa* represented for *manbo* Simplice to serve both the spirits and her clients. Soft light filtering in from doorways on each side heightens the feelings evoked in worshipers quietly standing in front of this healing but potentially volatile array. In Haiti, altars are the crossroads of life and death, where the past and the future and the spirit and mortal worlds converge. A refuge of hope, optimism, and healing, "cosmic cockpits" like *manbo* Simplice's honor the long history of African, European, and Native American influences in Haiti, but also meet the evolving needs of contemporary believers in Vodou.

—MARILYN HOULBERG

Kalfou
Crossroads

KALFOU DANJERE (DANGEROUS CROSSROADS)

—BOUKMAN EKSPERYANS

O wou o, kalfou nèg Kongo
Si ou touye, ou chaje ak pwoblèm
Nan kalfou, kalfou nèg Kongo
Si ou vole, ou chaje ak pwoblèm
Nan kalfou, kalfou nèg Kongo

* * *

O wou o, kalfou nèg Kongo
Magouyé, ou chaje ak pwoblèm
Nan kalfou, kalfou nèg Kongo

* * *

Ou manti, ou chaje ak pwoblèm
Nan kalfou, kalfou nèg Kongo
O wou o, kalfou nèg Kongo.

O wou o, crossroads of the Kongo people
If you kill, you'll be in deep trouble
At the crossroads of the Kongo people
If you steal, you'll be in deep trouble
At the crossroads, at the crossroads
    of the Kongo people

* * *

O wou o, crossroads of the Kongo people
Deceivers, you'll be in deep trouble
At the crossroads, the crossroads of
    the Kongo people

* * *

Liars, you'll be in deep trouble
At the crossroads, the crossroads of
    the Kongo people
O wou o, crossroads of the Kongo people

In this song, *Kalfou Danjere*, the Haitian musical group Boukman Eksperyans celebrates the powerful intersection of forces at the crossroads. The recording features songs that protest the military regime that ousted the country's first democratically elected president, Jean-Bertrand Aristide. All who kill, lie, cheat, or steal, the lyrics warn, will be judged at the crossroads.

The crossroads is the sacred space where the human and divine worlds intersect. Here, mortals may contact *les invisibles*, the source of life, and cosmic memory.

The crossroads concept is associated with

Ounfò *of oungan Guy Bata in Léogâne.*

*Vèvè **honoring Kalfou, the sacred crossroads. Vodouists use** vèvè,
or symbolic ritual drawings, to invoke the lwa.*

the Kongo people of Central Africa. The ancient motif they used to represent the cosmic intersection—the cruciform—was already a part of everyday life in many parts of Africa when fifteenth-century Portuguese Christians set up their missions in present-day Congo. But while the Kongo cosmogram paralleled the Christian crucifix in form, it neither evoked the tragic execution of a martyr nor carried any connotation of agony and suffering. Instead—like the sacred four directions in southwest Native American cultures—the crossroads spans the length and breadth of the universe with two roads that flow into and strengthen one another.

In the sixteenth century, African captives

of the slave trade brought the concept of the crossroads with them to Haiti, where it became known as *kalfou* (from the French *carrefour*). As in Africa today, the crossroads are guarded by the trickster spirit Legba, who must be honored before other *lwa* at rituals and ceremonies or before any important undertaking.

The theme of the crossroads has been passed down from Africa to Haiti to the American South through Vodou and Hoodoo culture. References to it surface in the lyrics of African-American musicians, from blues singers such as Robert Johnson in the 1930s to contemporary artists such as the Neville Brothers of Louisiana.

In Haitian Vodou, the Kongo cosmogram of the crossroads appears in numerous contexts. It is traced in the air as a servitor holds up a sequined Vodou bottle or other offering and salutes the four cardinal points. It is drawn on the ground with cornmeal and other substances to form *vèvè*, the ground drawings that serve to invite the *lwa* to descend and join the ceremony. It is painted on Vodou temple walls. It is worn on sequined *rara* jackets when Vodouists celebrate the spring festival of *rara* and do cosmic battle at the crossroads with magical powders that are blown in the four directions. It is also the symbol of Papa Legba, the guardian of the crossroads, the place of chance and change.

This altar is in honor of the Vodou *lwa* of the crossroads and intersections, Kalfou. It is located at the entrance to the sacred space of the Vodou temple of *oungan* Guy Bata of Léogâne, on the Kalfou Road, leading west out of Port-au-Prince. It is situated at both a physical and spiritual crossroads. Kalfou is the Petwo, or "hot," equivalent of Papa Legba—the paradoxical trickster who inhabits the crossroads and is known as the one who "opens the spiritual way." Typically, he has his own shrine, separate from the larger temple. In this powerful image, his piercing red eyes and red hands signal his hot, dynamic energy. The Barbancourt rum bottle tied to his body further signifies his hot nature. His gray hair alludes to his age, as an aspect of the wisdom of old Papa Legba. The rope/whip around his neck and the medicine bundle on his head suggest he stands as an empowered spirit, well equipped to adjudicate the affairs of the crossroads. He guards the entrance to the *ounfò*.

—MARILYN HOULBERG

Kabann Lwa
Spirit Bed

In most *ounfò,* a special room with a bed is dedicated to the major *lwa* served by the Vodou society. The *oungan* or *manbo* sleeps there on certain days to receive special messages from the *lwa.* This room and bed function as a *repozwa* or dwelling place for the *lwa,* and as such are kept in immaculate condition, as the *lwa* favor cleanliness. The room and bed may also be used as a guest room for distinguished visitors on special occasions.

A spirit bed in Souvenance for the lwa *Kebyesou; people seek out this* lwa *when they are sick.*

Poto Mitan

Sacred Centerpost

Within many *ounfò* is a *poto mitan*, or centerpost, a pillar extending from floor to ceiling; this is the path the *lwa* take from the ancestral spirit world of Ginen to the earthly world.

Ginen is also Guinea—ancient West Africa. It was from the Gulf of Guinea that many slaves were shipped to the Americas, and in the tradition of Vodou that shore is utterly lost and irretrievable—the stuff of legend. *Lwa* also made the journey from Africa to the Caribbean in the time of slavery.

Madame Micheline of Port-au-Prince, dressed in ritual white, sits in her ounfò *alongside the* poto mitan.

Oungan *Volny Derosier in his ounfò in La Petite Rivière. This chain, like a poto mitan, represents the path spirits travel from Ginen to the world of the living.*

Afè Vodou

SYMBOLS AND RITUAL OBJECTS

Everything I'm going to tell you is history. You have to go back to the beginning to get to the flags....*Manbo* Ayizan is the queen of Vodou—she was the first to present Vodou. All the *lwa* lived with her but they were not yet enlightened. They didn't know who they were or what they were supposed to do. It was long, long ago. They all lived in *manbo* Ayizan's house because she was the most powerful, the mother of all *oungan* who watched over everyone in the *djevo* and knew how to serve the spirits. Then Papa Loko, who is responsible for the *ason*, began a revolt. Papa Danbala followed him and went to live in a palm tree where he turned into a snake. Agwe Tawoyo turned into a fish and commanded the sea....Each *lwa* who revolted took responsibility for something, symbolized something. They filed out of *manbo* Ayizan's house one by one. Then Papa Sobo said, yes, I am going to make a flag. He took a bit of wood, he put a little cloth on it and said, yes, there, there is going to be a flag for signaling all the *lwa*. Now he's the one responsible for the flag, he's the master of the flag. He made one white flag, one red flag...peace, victory.

—From an interview with *oungan*/flagmaker CLOTAIRE BAZILE,
by Anna Wexler

Léogâne. Rose Anne and Andre Rose Mercilien, with drapo *(ritual flags)*
for Ogou Feray and Saint James the Greater. A vèvè depicting
Danbala, Ayida Wèdo, and Ayizan is on the floor.

Ason

Ritual Rattles

*T*he Vodou priestess, citizen of ancient Guinea, stands shrouded within the protective veil of a ritual flag. Fixed in her hand is the sacred symbol of her religious authority, the beaded calabash *ason* and the hand bell, her musical telecommunications device within the divine world of the *lwa*.

The *ason* is the bell–snake tongue of Dambala Wèdo, the great cosmic serpent and creator of all life forms. In the hand of the priestess, it is a vessel of power, a magic gourd-wand that can release great astral power, affording her a measure of control over *les mystères*. The encasing web of rainbow colored beads represents snake vertebrae of Dambala Wèdo. Each vertebra, in turn, represents a fertilizing life seed. Dambala Wèdo, who is associated with the Roman Catholic Saint Patrick, never speaks at Vodou ceremonies. Instead, those possessed during ritual events by this *lwa* emit hissing sounds in the ancient language of the eternal serpent.

—SAL SCALORA

Detail of ason, *or ritual rattles, from the wall of an abandoned* ounfò.

Take the *ason*. This sacred rattle is not
    a toy!
Ason, ason, ason speaks the
    language!
Show the magic rite way to me, to us,
    to all the children.
Sacred *ason! Ason!*
Open the way of the mysteries for me,
    for us, for all African children.
For the right hand, for the left hand,
    that they may serve well all
    humanity.
So that East and West may meet.

—THEODORE (LÒLÒ) BEAUBRUN

Poeling Leme of Port-au-Prince holds an ason, *or ritual rattle, the "tongue of Danbala" and traditional emblem of the* oungan's *power within the Rada tradition of Vodou. When an* oungan *or* manbo *ascends to the priesthood, he or she is said to have "taken the* ason."

Govi

Pots to House the Spirits

In Vodou belief and practice, a person has two souls, or sources of consciousness, known as *ti bon anj* (lesser soul) and *gwo bon anj* (greater soul). More stable, the lesser soul may return to God after death, while the greater soul wanders without rest. It is this more vulnerable greater soul that, it is said, can be captured. In the case of an initiate who has died, the greater soul must be put in a proper resting place such as a *govi*. *Govi* are terracotta pots, often wrapped in cloth, that house the spirits of the dead.

Altar, with govi, *in the* ounfò *of Necle Theus.*

Oungan *Samson Xavier Emperor La Count stands beside govi clustered on a community altar in the village of Badjo in the Artibonite Valley.*

Pakèt Kongo
Spirit Bundles

Pakèt kongo, or spirit-activated healing bundles, consist of curative herbs wrapped in cloth, crisscrossed with colorful satin ribbons held in place with straight pins, and topped with feathers. They amplify the healing nature of Vodou. *Pakèt* with arms akimbo are considered female; those with a vertical stem are male. After having been "heated up" through fire rituals, these *pakèt kongo* work together to effect their cures, frequently in the name of Simbi Andezo, the water spirit associated with healing medicines.

—MARILYN HOULBERG

Oungan *Volny Derosier of La Petite Rivière. A large* pakèt kongo *stands in front of him.*

Drapo
Flags

Ritual flags are among the most important objects of Vodou sacred art and ceremony. Each Vodou society has its own cherished *drapo* which stand within the *ounfò*. The flags are important parts of ceremonies, and they are carried through the streets during the *rara* ceremonies of spring, when members of the various societies take to the streets with music and dancing.

> *Papa se nou-e delege*
> *Pale kò drapo-a pou mwen*
> *Si na dako-e*
> *Wèdo rele Wèdo*
> *Wèdo rele Wèdo la*
> *Nou prale wè*
> *Si na dako-e*

> Papa that's us, delegates
> Speak to the flag-bearers for me
> If we will agree
> Wèdo call Wèdo
> Wèdo call Wèdo here
> We are going to see
> If we can agree

Older *drapo*—and those still made in the countryside—are fashioned of plain fabric in brilliant colors; modern *drapo*, made of luxurious fabrics like satin or velvet, are elaborately embroidered with sequins and beads in gorgeous colors. Each *drapo* is dedicated to a specific *lwa*, and often depicts the *lwa's* colors and symbols, including the spirit's *vèvè*, or cosmogram, or the Catholic saint who is associated with the *lwa*. Like brilliant quilts, *drapo* are often designed in geometric patterns, with patches of deep and bright color overstitched with appliqués and bordered by lush fringes of colored threads.

Drapo are also among the symbols of Vodou that most powerfully weave together political, spiritual, and historical meanings. Their origin is not certain, but many scholars believe that *drapo* evolved from either West African flag traditions or European military flags—or both. In both continents, flags symbolized force and power: They were the possessions of kings and leaders and were carried in the vanguards of armies. Vodou flags continue to signify the unity of their societies and the respect those societies hold for the power of the *lwa*.

Manbo *Notreda Antoine of Jacmel stands before the white* drapo
of peace and the red drapo *of victory.*

Vèvè

Ritual Drawings

Vèvè, or sacred ground drawings, are the joint legacy of the indigenous peoples of Haiti, the Taino-Arawak and the Carib, and certain African ethnic groups, such as the Edo of Nigeria. The Edo use these drawings as Haitians do: Each *lwa* has an intricate *vèvè* design that recalls the spirit's unique characteristics and is used to invoke the *lwa*.

While *vèvè* have inspired outstanding paintings by celebrated Haitian artists such as Castera Bazile, Wilson Bigaud, Enouch Placide, and André Pierre, one can see them painted on the walls of most *ounfò* or Vodou temples. In the *vèvè*, one also finds a legacy of Freemasonic symbols (known as *pwen*), which further illustrates the all-inclusiveness of Vodou.

***Vèvè** for Ezili*

VÈVÈ

Bèl nègès tout an blan,
(de pijon, de toutrèl)
bèl hounsi inosan,
ti nègès rèn-chantrèl,
pla men'w se oun vèvè
kote tout liny kontre:
liny tèr kwaze liny kè
liny fòs fonn ak liny chans.

Pla men'w se oun vèvè
kot lavi pa gen bout,
kot syèl ak tè fè youn,
kot lespri tounen moun.
Pla men'w se oun vèvè
lanmou san desepsyon,
kot tou sa ki pèdi
tounen jwenn direksyon.

Black woman, all in white,
(dove of love, dove of peace)
ounsi of innocence,
beautiful queen of songs,
your palm is a *vèvè*,
a point where all lines touch:
where the lines from the mind
meet the lines from the heart,
and the lines of courage
cross those of destiny.

Your palm is a *vèvè*
where life is limitless,
heaven and earth are one,
the spirits are human.
Your palm is a *vèvè*
of the most faithful love,
a place where all lost souls
can find new directions.

—SERGE MADHERE

Madame Micheline as Azaka, with a vèvè for Ezili.

Tanbou

Sacred Drums

Drums are the soul of Haitian Vodou—indeed, the word *Vodou* means "drum and spirits." Vodou drums are conical or goblet-shaped, varying in size and structural detail according to their purpose. For rituals in the Rada tradition, they are played in a set of three, and are covered with cowhide and tuned with pegs driven into the body of each drum. Drummers use sticks and their bare hands to achieve the proper sounds. Cowhide is required to withstand the heavy blows of the master drummer. During the Petwo rite, the drums appear in a set of two (sometimes a third small drum—called *kata* because of the sound it makes when played with two small sticks—may be added). Their goatskin drumheads are tightened with cords and played with bare hands.

Practitioner *Pouchon stands beside a Rada* manman tanbou *(lead drum). Behind him is a mural of Saint James.*

*Silva Joseph of Port-au-Prince as Ogou Achade. Beside him are
three Rada drums and, behind his right arm, a Petwo drum.*

Imaj
Images of Catholic Saints

Over time, Catholic images, prayers, and icons have become integral parts of Vodou worship in Haiti. Scholars debate whether such inclusion represented a real integration of Catholic saints and rituals into Vodou practice, or whether it was a means to cloak the Vodou practitioners' real spirituality from hostile authorities.

Visible evidence of syncretism can be observed in the use of depictions of Catholic saints to refer to the *lwa* or Vodou spiritual entities: Saint Patrick, the bishop who chased the snakes out of Ireland, is conflated with Danbala, the royal serpent of the Fon of Dahomey; and the French crusader Saint James the Greater represents Ogou Feray, deity of iron and war. Still other Catholic personages, such as Our Lady of Perpetual Help, whose image is found in many *ounfò*, or Vodou temples, have no corresponding *lwa* in Vodou liturgy.

Painting of Saint Peter, associated with Papa Legba, guardian of the threshold between the spirit and material worlds.

Saint John the Baptist is linked to Ogou Chango, lwa of luck. Mural from the ounfò of manbo Ima Plesimond in Port-au-Prince.

Pope
Dolls

Dolls are mysterious figures, evoking feelings of fear and dread as frequently as those of adoration. The most evocative of all dolls is the infamous voodoo doll. Standing as the foremost icon of New World African-based religions in the mind of the Western world, the "voodoo doll" is the incarnation of the vast misconceptions and misrepresentations surrounding these faiths. The image of a doll jabbed full of pins, designed for malevolent purposes, is a potent yet grossly simplified caricature of the doll/figures that are used in these religions, which include Haitian Vodou and Cuban Santeria. These doll/figures and their antecedents, Kongo *minkisi*, Dahomean *bocio* figures, and Haitian *pakèt kongo*, among others, are as often made for directing healing energy as they are for the catharsis of charged emotions such as anger and revenge. From the *ibeji* twin figures of Yorubaland, who represent deceased children, to the baby doll representations of the saints/spirits in Haiti, Cuba, and Brazil, to the soft, stuffed doll/figures used as *pwen* or points of spiritual/magical concentration in Haitian Vodou and Louisiana Hoodoo, these doll/figures serve a variety of subtle yet powerful functions. The "doll," a figure which stands at the crossroads of the living and the collective dead or ancestral spirits, is called upon to act as mediator, being both a vessel of negotiation and a mirror of divine complexity.

—ALISON LAIRD CRAIG

Dolls in the ounfò *of St. Louis Bata.*

76

Altar for Ezili created by manbo *Madame Celanie Constant Nerva of Jacmel, featuring a number of dolls.*

Sèvitè

PRACTITIONERS

It has been said that Vodou is not so much a religion as a practice: This is not to downplay the spiritual importance of the tradition, but to emphasize the importance of active service rather than passive belief in Vodou spirituality. Followers of Vodou do not identify themselves as "Vodouists," as adherents of the Catholic church would say they are "Catholics." Rather, they say they are "servants of the spirits."

Within a Vodou society, or *sosyete*, there is a hierarchy of service. The leader of an *ounfò* or temple is the *oungan* (priest) or *manbo* (priestess). He or she is intimate with the ways of the *lwa*, the spirits; Vodou priests not only lead ceremonies honoring the *lwa*, they also interpret problems brought about by spiritual interference in the lives of their followers and intercede with the *lwa* when a petitioner needs specific help, as with love or work. A certain kind of *oungan* is known as *bòkò*, or sorcerer. These men are said to practice "with both hands": one hand to serve the *lwa*, the other to work magic.

In the service of the temple, and in the conduct of ceremonies, other members of the society have specific roles and offices, too. Chief among these are the *ounsi*, or initiates, who perform as a sort of chorus, singing and dancing. The *ounsi* also participate in the various rituals.

Ereniche Jilium of St. Marc, dressed as Ezili Freda,
sits atop a spirit bed for Ezili, the lwa *of love.*

Oungan
Priest

*H*ow does a man know that he has been called? It usually begins in troubled dreams. At first his dreams are vague. He is visited by a strange being which he cannot identify. He cannot make out at first what is wanted of him. He touches rich fabrics momentarily but they flit away from his grasp. Strange perfumes wisp across his face, but he cannot know where they came from, nor find a name out of his memory for them. The dream visitations become more frequent and definite and sometimes Erzulie identifies herself definitely. But more often, the matter is more elusive. He falls ill, other unhappy things befall him. Finally his friends urge him to visit a *houngan* for a consultation. Quickly then, the visitor is identified as the goddess of love and the young man is told that he has been having bad luck because the goddess is angry at his neglect. She behaves like any other female when she is spurned. A baptism is advised and a "service" is instituted for the offended *loa* and she is placated and the young man's ill fortune ceases.

—Zora Neale Hurston,
Tell My Horse

Alexi Gangan Bienconnu of the Artibonite Valley is an important oungan—even his name, "Gangan Bienconnu," describes him as well known.

Remèd
Medicine

Many *oungan* and *manbo* are also doctors with great knowledge of herbal medicine. Throughout Haiti, folk medicine is one of the primary sources of medical care for many. And as the Western medical establishment begins to officially recognize herbal medicine, the widespread knowledge of native herbs that many Haitians possess is finally being valued.

Marie Lily Cerat said Vodou is "the religion that taught my ancestors of the past and the present about self-discipline, self-worth, and self-esteem" and that Vodou provides "many of the services freely [that] people pay psychologists big money for." Here, Cerat recalls a ceremony.

A woman sorts herbs in the ounfò *of Ima Plesimond.*

A wooden pail was filled with mortared leaves in a mixture of Florida water, holy water and *kleren* [Haitian white rum] and would sit for three days. The leaves would rot and the aroma would become unbearable although it was covered under a white muslin sheet. This mixture would bathe all the people in the family. And it would be on the eve of the night when the invisible white man in the North Pole would fly by with gifts for little children whose houses had chimneys. Indeed, the North Pole was far from Haiti. So he was not the talk of the day for most of the people where I was. Giving foods to the "spiritual guards of our bodies" was the most important event. And Francine, like an automaton, repeated these rituals year after year each December 24.

On that day, we would drink the red blood of the turtle and chicken; we would also be eating it that day, mixed with herbs. Reluctantly, we would be bathed by Francine, the matriarch of the family, in the pungent herbal blend, drink the blood and herb mixture, and rush to the floor where the meal was served on freshly cut banana leaves. The ultimate reward. Did it accomplish its purpose? Yes. After being told that this ceremony was meant to guide us to face

A child waits to receive medicines from oungan *Jean Philippe Jeannot.*

our responsibilities toward ourselves and the community, it rendered us stronger. It accomplished the psychological work.

Though it suffers all the problems and more that cause people in wealthy, industrialized countries to search out therapies or completely go crazy, the truth is that Haiti has very few mental institutions. Vodou provides us Haitians with many channels to filter our frustrations, our problems, and even our sexual ambivalence. Indeed, Vodou has proven so effective in this way, that psychologists and therapists in Haiti must have "back-up" jobs.

—MARIE LILY CERAT

Bòkò

Sorcerer

Bòkò ba ou pwen men l pa di ou domi gran chemen.

"The *bòkò* gives you a protective charm, but he doesn't tell you to sleep in the middle of the highway," warns this savvy Haitian proverb, collected by Harold Courlander in the 1950s. Along with its commonsense message, the adage also reveals the key role in Haitian society of the *bòkò*, a Vodou priest who is said to "work with both hands"—for both creation and destruction. The *bòkò* is feared for his magical powers, but he can also provide protection from anyone dispensing harmful magic. He makes protective amulets but can also send spirits to wreak havoc on his clients' enemies.

The *bòkò* uses magic and communicates with the *lwa*, as well as the dead. He is also closely associated with Bizango, a secret society that is most active between midnight and dawn.

—MARILYN HOULBERG

Though he is a young oungan, *St. Louis Bata's demeanor is intimidating, which only adds to his reputation as a powerful* bòkò.

84

Zonbi

Zombiism

From Haitian folklore to travelers' logs to rumor, once the popular media caught hold of the gruesome Haitian legend of the zombie, it ran wild with it. The zombie phenomenon became standard fodder for horror films of the 1930s, '40s, '50s, and '60s. As a result, for outsiders today, the zombie is probably the most persistent association with Haitian Vodou.

How real is the zombie phenomenon—are there "living dead" roaming the Haitian countryside? The answer is complex, made more so because in Vodou practice, the term *zombie* itself has multiple meanings. In Haiti, the making of "zombies" lies within the jurisdiction of the *bòkò*, the sorcerer-priest said to "work with both hands," for creative and destructive ends. In common Vodou parlance, however, to "make a zombie" of someone simply means capturing that person's spirit after they have died to force it to do the bidding of the *bòkò*. Even this more ethereal bondage leads to the ironic arrangement in which, as one observer put it, the *bòkò*, "the descendant of slaves becomes the slaveholder."

Reported sightings of actual "living dead" in Haitian marketplaces and obscure corners of the countryside occur, but rarely. When they do, rumors run like wildfire, pounced upon and worked over and over by the local newspapers and radio broadcasts. How grounded in reality these reports are is up for debate.

Still, the powder used to turn people into zombies does exist. The drug, a composition of herbs and animal products, diminishes a person's vital signs; having ingested it, a person requires very little oxygen and can remain alive for up to forty-eight hours. Haitian tradition holds that people dug up and brought back as zombies—alive but mentally impaired by a lack of oxygen flow to the brain after being buried underground—were used as slaves to labor on Haiti's vast sugar plantations.

Haitian folklore cites seven transgressions that warrant turning a person into a zombie: Among these are adultery and stealing title to land. Some say that in colonial times zombification was used as retribution against a landed elite who usurped meager peasant holdings—the only means of survival for the rural poor. Doubtless, though, zombification has also been used as a weapon for simple personal vendetta.

Bòkò *driving two* zonbi. *Painting on the wall of an* ounfò.

Sosyete
Secret Societies

Haiti's Bizango and Makanda secret societies have sensationalized, unwarranted reputations as criminals who eat children and turn humans into zombies. Their dark reputations arose chiefly because little is known about them. Actually, these societies function to strengthen and protect their communities. Elders in the societies, who carry the titles of "emperor" or "empress," are among the most knowledgeable people in their neighborhoods, keeping alive the traditions of Haitian society and culture. These societies have their origins in the slave communities of colonial Haiti, where they served as a secret countervailing force to the system within which the Afro-Haitians found themselves trapped.

Mural on the wall of an *ounfò*, Point Sonde.
Members of Bizango are said to be able to transform
themselves into any animal they wish.

Oungan *Raoul Louis San, member of the Bizango secret society.*

Manbo
Priestess

You do the cards for a person. In the cards you see the problem of the person. But when a person come to see you he doesn't have anything to say. You have to read the cards. You're going to spread out the cards, to see what the person need. You explain it. You tell the person, "You came to see me because you are a person who is sick" or "You have a problem with a man." The cards tell you and then you speak with the person, and you ask, "What do you say?" And the person speaks to you and says: "What you say is true."

And for telling many other thing…if you see something in his face, you say, "Did this happen to you," "Did you have an accident," "Did you go to the hospital…?" They say, "Yes." You search to see if the accident was natural or not. You can have an accident that is natural. You can understand me? You can have a sickness that is natural. You see someone who is sick, you say to that person, "Why you have to waste money, because you better go to a doctor…because you do not have anything on you. Better go find a doctor, who can see truly what you have because these cards do not give an answer like you are sick because of something that was sent on you." You have people who have things "thrown on them" (*voye sou li*), but you have others who don't have that. It is a natural sickness they have, but people imagine that it is other people who have caused it. If someone has a *maladi* of the imagination, you can't do anything for them. You can survey someone's house…go there, read cards…you don't find a thing, because they have nothing. It is a doctor's sickness they have. But they have an imagination and think that someone has done bad against them. There are people like that, but there are also people who really do bad. So you search to find where a malady comes from.

—*Manbo* Mama Lola, from an interview with Karen McCarthy Brown in *Sacred Arts of Haitian Vodou*

Like many manbo, *Ima Plesimond of Port-au-Prince uses cards to divine the fate of her clients.*

90

Madame Celanie Constant Nerva of Jacmel holds her ason, *the badge of her power as a* manbo.

The one who has the *ason* must have self-control over her heart, and keep a cool head. She must make abnegation and be an altruist. She must serve the Ginen frankly. She must serve the mysteries. It is the priests, the *oungan* and *manbo*, who use the *ason*, because they have reached the grade that allows them to do so. One cannot buy such a grade with money. No man can give this grade to anyone. Only the Great Master, the Spirit, and the *lwa* may confer this grade on somebody.

—THEODORE (LÒLÒ) BEAUBRUN

Ounsi
Initiates

Ounsi have decided to become intimate for life with a particular *lwa*. Often, a person has a dream or an illness that leads him or her to choose initiation. It is said that an *ounsi* "dies and is reborn" in the process of initiation, which lasts a week, or sometimes two. The goal of the initiation ritual is to bind the initiate permanently with a *lwa*, who is believed to be lodged in the head of the *ounsi* until his or her death. With this close partnership, the *ounsi* gains deeper understanding of the ways of the spirits and is empowered to participate in ceremonies in their honor.

*E*verything went wrong, small things (lost keys, jammed doors, mail that did not arrive) and big ones. The trouble started when the heating pipes froze and burst in January. Less than two weeks later, Maggie lost her job and contracted chicken pox. The bad luck then began to spread, as it is known to do, to vulnerable others (those not spiritually protected) who were connected to them. Gabriel, Alourdes's former boyfriend, who was living with them at the time, was mugged. Alourdes's son William was arrested for purse snatching.

When bad luck is pervasive, "you got to pay attention to that," as Alourdes put it. But in order to pay attention, a person has to be centered and calm enough to sleep well, dream frequently, and remember those dreams. By early March, the anxiety level in the house had risen so high that when the spirits sent Maggie a dream warning her about the next link in the chain of bad luck, she did not remember it right away, and, when she did remember, she misinterpreted a key element:

They warn me. They tell me about that. I just have too many thing in my head. I forget about it. I just been running around trying to do too many thing. But I dream....I dream that I come home one night and find my door open, and I go in there and look, and there are four horses looking at me right from the fire escape. They just standing there looking at me, and then I hear something in the front of my apartment, you know, in the bedroom, and I go in there...and there is Joe. You know Joe? Aileen's son. And I say to him, "What you doing in my apartment?" And he tell me he just come in looking for something. And I get real mad and just sock him, beat him up! And throw him out!

Ounsi *Sainte Anise Jn. Jacques, J. Damante Antoine, and
Victoire Avena belong to the same Vodou society in the village of Badjo.*

In mid-March, a few days after this dream, the row house in Fort Greene was robbed, the first burglary they had experienced in nearly twenty years of living there. Maggie occupies the second-floor apartment, below the one rented out to Aileen and her son, Joe. The burglar got onto the fire escape in back and came in through Maggie's kitchen window, where the horses were standing in her dream. Maggie lost the engagement ring that Raphael Sanchez, Michael's father, had given her; a jar full of quarters; a collection of foreign money; and a new camera for which she had yet to make her first payment....Maggie had not realized how directly the spirits were speaking to her. The robbery clinched Maggie's diagnosis about the cause of the period of bad luck. She decided it was definitely a result of harassment by the spirits, who were demanding that she stop postponing her initiation. It had been almost two years since the important dream in which she had sworn to Danbala that she would return to Haiti to take the *ason*. Work and financial troubles, she said, had prevented her from fulfilling her promise right away....In fact, during the two years since her promise to Papa Danbala, Maggie had been struggling mightily with the consequences of taking on the responsibilities of a *manbo*.

—KAREN MCCARTHY BROWN, *Mama Lola: A Vodou Priestess in Brooklyn*

Portrait of ounsi *Paule of Souvenance.*

Manje-lwa
Food for the *Lwa*

Feeding the spirits is central to Vodou practice. The *lwa* all have certain foods they prefer to be offered, and these offerings are an important part of rituals welcoming them. It is often a reciprocal offering: Food is prepared for and offered to the spirit, then it may be consumed as a feast by the participants in a ritual. Azaka likes corn, bread, and brandy; Bawon Samdi prefers a black goat or a black hen; Danbala and Ayida Wèdo crave white foods—rice, milk, and eggs; and Ezili Freda, the coquette, loves delicacies of all kinds, as well as rice and chicken. Liquor is also an important offering; depending upon the *lwa*, fiery liquor or rum is preferred.

A wall mural depicting food for the spirits.

Ritual Menu for Ezili Dantò

Brown Rice with Black Peas: Boil half a pound dried black peas until done, about an hour. After the peas are cooked, remove them from the pot and retain the water. Fry the peas for a few minutes in oil in a separate pan with salt, scallions, garlic, hot and black peppers, parsley, and thyme. Cover one pound of brown rice with the water from the black peas and cook over medium heat until done, about 30 to 40 minutes. Mix rice and peas together.

Stewed Chicken: Marinate chicken pieces in a bowl in the juices of one lemon and half a sour orange, with salt, scallions, garlic, hot and black peppers, parsley, and thyme added. In a pan, sauté 2 or 3 chopped tomatoes. Add the chicken and brown in 2 or 3 tablespoons of oil. Boil the chicken and tomatoes in 1 cup of water for about 30 to 45 minutes, until the water evaporates and the chicken appears slightly fried. Stir in cut-up onions, one can of tomato paste, and 3/4 cup of water and cook over medium heat for one half hour.

Side Dishes: Boiled sweet white yams, boiled green plantains, tomatoes and watercress

Drink: 1 bottle sweet liqueur

Dessert: White cake decorated in her favorite colors, green and white.

Place all the dishes on the altar table, which has been decorated with love. Make a sacrifice of food, prayer, and drink. Once the *lwa* have eaten, share with friends and family.

Food for the lwa *painted on these temple walls depicts the notion of sacrifice.*

Sèvitè

Servitors

All adherents of Vodou are said to "serve the spirits."

Those unfamiliar with Haiti often question what part of the Haitian population is linked to Vodou practice. Yet the more pertinent question may be, who is not? A religion that sustained slaves, peasants, and the dispossessed, Vodou remains inextricably ingrained in national culture. And though the country's elite has sought to distance itself from association with Vodou—rarely a status-symbol for those eager to climb the social ladder—many members of the middle and upper classes, in time of need, patronize Vodou rituals and avail themselves of the advice and services of the *oungan* and *manbo*.

—Gerdès Fleurant

Portrait of Alenord J. Baptiste of Gonaïves.

In Soukri in the Artibonite Valley, servitor Homel Dorival with a ceremonial cup used in rituals and liquor for the lwa. The hole in which he stands is a very sacred space.

*I*F THE EARTH is a sphere, then the abyss below the earth is also its heavens; and the difference between them is no more than time, the time of the earth's turning. If the earth is a vast horizontal surface reflecting, invisibly, even for each man his own proper soul, then again, the abyss below the earth is also its heavens, and the difference between them is time, the time of an eye lifting and dropping. The sun-door and the tree-root are the same thing in the same place, seen now from below and now from above and named, by the seer, for the moment of seeing.

—MAYA DEREN, *Divine Horsemen:*
The Living Gods of Haiti

G L O S S A R Y

Mural depicting Agwe.

AGWE TAWOYO: *lwa* of the sea, who protects seafarers and conducts the dead to Ginen

ASOTÒ: huge ritual drum, originally from Dahomey

ASON [ASSON]: ceremonial rattle; symbol of the spiritual power of an *oungan* or *manbo*

AYIDA WÈDO: female divinity; wife of Danbala

Mural depicting Danbala Wèdo.

AYIZAN: female Rada *lwa* of markets and of the *ounfò*

AZAKA [AZAKE MEDE, ZAKA, KOUZEN ZAKA, PAPA ZAKA]: Rada spirit of agriculture

BADJI: sanctuary room

BAWON [BARON]: head of the Gede family, the spirits of the cemetery. Members of this family of *lwa* include Bawon Samdi, Bawon Lakwa, Bawon Simityè, and others

BIZANGO: a secret society

BÒKÒ [BOCOR]: an *oungan* who is expert in supernatural ways; a sorcerer who works "with both hands"—for both creation and destruction

BONDYÉ: the supreme deity of Haitian Vodou tradition; also known as Gran Mèt

Bosou [Bossou]: the bull *lwa;* a protective spirit usually associated with Petwo tradition

Chango: *lwa* of luck, associated with Saint John the Baptist

Dahomey: present-day Benin, in West Africa. *See also* Ginen

Danbala [Damballah, Damballa, Danballa, Danballa Wèdo]: Rada serpent spirit associated with water, rainbows, and wisdom

danse-lwa: an act of possession during a Vodou ritual

dezounen: rite during which the spirit attached to an initiate is separated from him or her, just before or after death

djevo: sanctuary room within an *ounfò*

drapo [drapeau]: ceremonial flag

Mural depicting Ezili Dantò.

Ezili Dantò [Erzulie Dantor]: mother/warrior spirit of the Petwo tradition, usually dark-skinned (in contrast to Ezili Freda) and associated with a character of fierce protectiveness. *Ezili Je Wouj,* literally "Ezili Red Eyes": a fierce manifestation of Ezili Dantò

Ezili Freda [Erzulie Freida]: Rada spirit of love and sensuality

Gede [Guedé]: trickster spirit(s) of the dead and of sexuality; guardian of children

Ginen [Ginee, Guinea]: West African ancestral home; Vodou term for things derived from West Africa (e.g., Rada rites)

govi: clay jar containing the spirit essence of a deceased servitor

Mural depicting Bosou.

Mural depicting Lasirenn.

GWO BON ANJ: of the two parts of the Vodou soul, the "greater" part; *gwo bon anj*, lingers by the grave after death, and can be caught

KALFOU [KAFOU]: crossroads

KALFOU [KAFOU]: *lwa* of the spiritual crossroads; the Petwo Legba

KAY-MISTÈ: "house of the mysteries"; a hut within the *ounfò*

KONNESANS: level of spirit knowledge

KOUZEN: "cousin"; term used to address Azaka

KREYÒL: the language spoken in Haiti

LAKOU: compound including temple and other sacred spaces. Traditionally, the land of the *lakou* is held in common by the community.

LASIRENN [LASYRENN, LA SIRÈNE, LASIRÈN]: feminine watery spirit, often depicted as a mermaid or whale, associated with water, the sea, mystery, and seduction; *Labalenn* (from the French *la baleine*, whale) is her sister-spirit

LEGBA [ATIBON LEGBA]: Rada guardian spirit of gates and doorways

LWA [LOA]: spirit, deity, divinity of the Vodou religion; *lwa achte*, a spirit "purchased" as insurance against misfortune; *manje-lwa*, feast for the *lwa*

MAKOUT: straw bag associated with Azaka

MANBO [MAMBO]: Vodou priestess; woman who has the highest level of *konnesans* or knowledge of the spirits

MARASA: the sacred twins

MAWU-LISA: all-pervasive spiritual entity of the Fon people of West Africa

MISTÈ [MYSTÈRE]: "mystery," a term designating divine forces; *see* lwa

OGOU [OGOUN]: a family of warrior spirits associated with a strong sense of justice. Includes Ogou Feray, Ogou Osany, Ogou Chango and Sen Jak Majè, (Saint James the Greater), among others

OUNFÒ [OUFO, OUNFOR, HOUNFOR]: Vodou temple

OUNSI [HOUNSI]: initiate; wife of the spirits; member of religious society who participates in rituals

OUNGAN [HOUNGAN]: Vodou priest; *see* manbo

PAKÈT KONGO [PAKÈT, PAQUETTE]: spirit-activated bundle

PAPA: "father"; term used to address Legba and other *lwa*

PERISTIL: dancing space within a Vodou temple

PETWO: one of two spirit pantheons dominant in Port-au-Prince Vodou; pantheon of "hot" spirits coming from the Kongo and New World slavery experience. Invoked by cracking whips, gunfire, pouring libation; *see also* Rada

POTÈT: pot that contains hair and nail clippings—and also the *gwo bon anj* or greater soul—of an initiate

POTO MITAN: a sacred post in the *peristil* through which the *lwa* arrive among human beings

PWEN: charm or supernatural force; magical, protective power

RADA: one of two spirit pantheons dominant in Port-au-Prince Vodou; pantheon of "cool" or "sweet" spirits originally from Ginen (West Africa); *see also* Petwo

RARA: bands of Vodou faithful, musicians, and dancers who parade through the streets around Easter time

SEN: saint; divinity; *lwa*

SÈVITÈ: servitor; in Vodou, one who serves the spirits

SIMBI ANDEZO: the *lwa* of fresh water; a powerful *lwa* primarily served in the Petwo tradition

SOSYETE: a Vodou society

TI BON ANJ: of the two parts of the Vodou soul, the "lesser" part; *ti bon anj* travels under the ocean to Ginen after death

VÈVÈ: symbolic drawing of the *lwa*, used to invoke the divinities. Often inscribed on the ground, on walls, or on banners or sketched in the air with a sword or an *ason* during a ceremony. *Vèvè* also refers to the food placed on the drawings. Also called *seremoni*

VODOU: literally, "the drum and spirits"; the majority religion of Haiti

WANGA: a work of magic

ZONBI: "zombie"; a member of the undead, who is "killed" and brought back to life under the control of a *bòkò*

Vèvè *for Ezili.*

BIBLIOGRAPHY

African Arts. *The Arts of Haitian Vodou.* Spring 1996, Vol. XXXIX, No 2, University of California, Los Angeles, CA.

Aperture 126. *Haiti: Feeding the Spirit.* Number One Hundred Twenty-six, Winter, 1992.

Blier, Suzanna Preston. *African Vodon: Art, Psychology and Power.* Chicago: University of Chicago Press, 1994.

Brown, Karen McCarthy. *Mama Lola: A Vodou Priestess in Brooklyn.* Berkeley: University of California Press, 1991.

———. "The Vèvè of Haitian Vodou: A Structural Analysis of Visual Imagery." Ph.D. dissertation, Temple University, 1976.

———. *From the Collection of the Davenport Museum of Art, Tracing the Spirit: Ethnographic Essays on Haitian Art.* Published by the Davenport Museum of Art, Davenport, Iowa, in association with the University of Washington. Seattle and London: University of Washington Press, 1995.

Cosentino, Donald J., ed. *Sacred Arts of Haitian Vodou.* Los Angeles, California: UCLA Fowler Museum of Cultural History, 1995.

Courlander, Harold. *The Drum and the Hoe: Life and Lore of the Haitian People.* Berkeley: University of California Press, 1960.

———. *The Bordeaux Narrative.* Albuquerque, NM: University of New Mexico Press, 1990.

Danticat, Edwidge and Jonathan Demme. *Island of Fire.* Nyack, NY: Kaliko Press, 1997.

Deren, Maya. *Divine Horsemen: The Living Gods of Haiti.* New York: Chelsea House, McPherson & Co.; Thames and Hudson 1953 edition, 1983.

Desmangles, Leslie G. *The Faces of the Gods, Vodou and Roman Catholicism in Haiti.* Chapel Hill and London: University of North Carolina Press, 1992.

Drewal, Henry John. "Performing the Other: Mami Wata Worship in Africa." *The Drama Review,* #118, Summer 1988.

Dunham, Katherine. *Island Possessed*. Garden City, NY: Doubleday & Co, 1969.

Fleurant, Gerdès. *Dancing Spirits: Rhythms and Rituals of Haitian Vodou, the Rada Rite*. Westport, CT: Greenwood Publishing Group, Inc., 1996.

Galembo, Phyllis. *Divine Inspiration: From Benin to Bahia*. Albuquerque: University of New Mexico Press, 1993.

Girouard, Tina. *Sequin Artists of Haiti*. New Orleans: Contemporary Arts Center, 1994.

Gray, John, ed. *Ashe, Traditional Religion and Healing in Sub-Saharan Africa and the Diaspora: A Classified International Bibliography*. Westport, CT: Greenwood Press, 1989.

Hurbon, Laënnec. *Voodoo: Search for the Spirit, Discoveries*. New York: Harry Abrams Inc. Publishers, 1995.

Hurston, Zora Neale. *Tell My Horse*. Philadelphia: J.B. Lippincott, 1938.

Métraux, Alfred. *Voodoo in Haiti*. Translated by Hugo Charteris. New York: Oxford University Press, (Schocken Books) 1959 (1972).

Rodman, Selden. *Where Art is Joy, Haitian Art: The First Forty Years*. Randolph, NH: Ruggles de Latour, Inc., 1988.

——— and Carol Cleaver. *Spirits of the Night, the Vaudun Gods of Haiti*. Dallas: Spring Publications, 1992.

Rowell, Charles H., ed. *Callaloo, Haiti: The Literature and Culture*, Part I, Vol. 15 #2; Part II, Vol. 15 #3. Baltimore, MD: The Johns Hopkins University Press, 1992.

Thompson, Robert Farris. *Face of the Gods: Art and Altars of Africa and the African Americas*. New York and Munich: Museum for African Art; Prestel 1993.

———. *Flash of the Spirit: African and Afro-American Art and Philosphy*. New York: Random House, 1983.

TontonGuy, ed. *Tanbou: Revue Haïtienne d'Études Politiques et Littéraires*. Brookline, MA.

Wexler, Anna. "For the Flower of Ginen: The Artistry of Clotaire Bazile, a Haitian Vodou Flagmaker." Ph.D. dissertation, Harvard University, 1997.

Wilcken, Lois. *The Drums of Vodou*. Tempe, AZ: White Cliffs Media Co., 1992.

Wolkstein, Diane. *The Magic Orange Tree and Other Haitian Folktales*. New York: Schocken Books, 1978, 1997.

Yih, Y.-M. David. "Music and Dance of Haitian Vodou: Diversity and Unity in Regional Repertoires." Ph.D. dissertation, Wesleyan University, 1995.

DISCOGRAPHY

Angels in the Mirror: Vodou Music of Haiti. Ellipsis Arts ISBN 1-55961-387-4.

Boukan Ginen. *Jou A Rive.* Xenophile 4024, 1995.

Boukman Eksperyans. *Libete.* Mango 162-539, 9462, 1995.

Caribbean Revels: Haitian Rara and Dominican Gaga. Recordings by Verna Gillis, notes by Verna Gillis and Gage Averill. 1991. Smithsonian Folkways CD 40202.

Divine Horsemen: The Voodoo Gods of Haiti. Recordings by Maya Deren. Produced by Teiji Ito and Cheryl Ito. 1980 Lyrichord. Disc. Inc. LLST 7341.

The Drums of Vodou. Featuring Frisner Augustin and La Troupe Makandal (cassette and CD). Recorded by The Place Recording Studios and Skunk Hollow Studio. Produced by White Cliffs Media Company. 1992 (cassette), 1994 (CD).

Erzili. Featuring La Troupe Makandal with Master Drummer Frisner Augustin. Recorded by Harry Leroy. Cassette produced by World Music Institute. 1994 WMI 019.

Mambo Lucienne. *Reine Du Voodou.* J.J. Hogarth PAP JJ100.

Music of Haiti, Vols. I-III (Folk Music of Haiti/Drums of Haiti/Songs and Dances of Haiti). Recordings and notes by Harold Courlander. Smithsonian Folkways. 1952.

Rhythms of Rapture: Sacred Music of Haitian Vodou. Smithsonian Folkways 40464.

Roots of Haiti Voodoo. Many Volumes of Mini Records MRSD 1063.

Ti Roro. *Haitian Drummer.* Cook 05004.

Ti Roro. *Roots of Haiti.* Mini Records, MRS 1066 vol.4, 1979.

Wawa and Azor Collections 8 & 3 and 9 & 1. Geronimo Records GR 0014-79.

Zobop. Editions "R" PAP, STR-10008.